Breaking the Development Logjam

NEW STRATEGIES FOR BUILDING COMMUNITY SUPPORT

DOUGLAS R. PORTER

ULI–the Urban Land Institute
1025 Thomas Jefferson Street, N.W.
Suite 500 West
Washington, D.C. 20007-5201
http://www.uli.org

Library of Congress Cataloging-in-Publication Data
Porter, Douglas R.
Breaking the development logjam : new strategies for building community support / Douglas R. Porter.
p. cm.
ISBN-13: 978-0-87420-956-3
1. Community development. 2. City planning—Citizen participation. 3. Sustainable development. I. Title.
HN49.C6P67 2006
307.1'2160973—dc22 2006036078

ISBN: 978-0-87420-956-3

10 9 8 7 6 5 4 3 2 1

Printed in the United States of America.

About ULI–the Urban Land Institute

ULI–the Urban Land Institute is a nonprofit education and research institute that is supported by its members. Its mission is to provide responsible leadership in the use of land in order to enhance the total environment.

ULI sponsors education programs and forums to encourage an open international exchange of ideas and sharing of experiences; initiates research that anticipates emerging land use trends and issues and proposes creative solutions based on that research; provides advisory services; and publishes a wide variety of materials to disseminate information on land use and development. Established in 1936, the Institute today has more than 28,000 members from 80 countries, representing the entire spectrum of the land use and development disciplines. The Institute is recognized throughout the world as one of America's most respected and widely quoted sources of objective information on urban planning, growth, and development.

Project Staff

Rachelle L. Levitt
Executive Vice President, Policy and Practice
Publisher

Marta V. Goldsmith
Senior Vice President, Community Outreach

Gayle Berens
Vice President, Real Estate Development Practice

Suzanne D. Cartwright
Director, Community Outreach, Land Use Programs
Project Director

Nancy H. Stewart
Director, Book Program
Managing Editor

Lori Hatcher
Director, Publications Marketing

James A. Mulligan
Associate Editor

Micaela Porta, Engine Books
Manuscript Editor

Betsy VanBuskirk
Art Director

Anne Morgan
Graphic Artist

Craig Chapman
Director, Publishing Operations

Acknowledgments

Several sources of information about community engagement processes were especially helpful in preparing this publication. One was a report authored by Kenneth Schreiber, Gary Binger, and Dennis Church, *Higher-Density Plans: Tools for Community Engagement,* for the Mineta Transportation Institute at San José State University with funding support from the California Department of Transportation and the U.S. Department of Transportation Research and Special Programs Administration. The report's discussions of the tools and techniques currently being used to gain community acceptance of proposed developments provided a useful reference and guide for the contents of this book. Of particular value were descriptions of specific visualization tools and resources that, with some editing, have been incorporated in this book by permission of the Mineta Transportation Institute.

The second helpful source was *Pulling Together: A Planning and Development Consensus-Building Manual,* published by ULI in 1994 in cooperation with several other organizations. Having prepared one of the case studies for the book, I was familiar with its contents. *Pulling Together*'s explanations of the various forms of engagement processes and the approaches that can be employed to reach consensus with community groups provided a thoughtful foundation for this publication.

The third and perhaps most important source of information for this publication was the group of seven case studies undertaken to detail the practices now being used in engagement and outreach processes. These studies not only told me what types of events led to agreements on development plans, but let me discuss with the process leaders their intentions and reflections on what happened and why. The leaders of these processes are the professionals who are pioneering effective approaches to community engagement—each bringing a somewhat different perspective on effective ways to meet the challenges. As always, for me, examining actual experience was an invaluable aid to understanding what really happens and why it works in these locales. My thanks to the people who offered information freely from their experience; their input is acknowledged in the individual studies.

Special mention is due Debra Stein, who has previously written on this subject for ULI. She was gracious enough to revise several text boxes borrowed from her Web site to include in this publication. As always, her lively style and practical information add value. Also, my thanks to the ULI staff that coaxed my efforts along to the finish line, especially Suzanne Cartwright, the project manager, and Marta Goldsmith, senior vice president for community outreach. Both were patient and helpful in getting it right. I'm also grateful for the insights offered by the four reviewers of the manuscript—Roger Galatas, Cales Givens, Frank Martin, and Frank Turner: two developers, a planning and design consultant, and a planning director, all with lengthy experience in the trenches of community engagement. Every author should have such help!

—Douglas R. Porter

Preface

Neighbors of proposed development projects often have strong opinions about them, especially concerning potential effects on their quality of life or property values. They can be critical of certain features or fearful of the whole concept of additional development in the area. Or they can be supportive of a project if the planned uses and design will improve some aspect of their neighborhood. Too often, citizens' reactions to proposed development rely on incomplete or mistaken information. Developers' advocacy for change tends to stir resentment and concerns among people who have become comfortable with the way things are.

The single most important step developers can take to minimize opposition to their proposals is to reach out to the community by informing citizens about the positive consequences of proposed projects. By engaging community residents and public officials in discussions about project plans and designs, developers can generate goodwill and a welcoming spirit. It is even possible that the ideas of participants in such processes can improve the quality of the development, benefiting the developer as well as the neighborhood and community.

Engaging the community in learning about prospective developments and in taking part in project planning and design builds a vested interest in the outcome and alters the dynamic of neighborhood and community attitudes from adversarial reaction to constructive involvement. Community engagement can be designed to promote high-quality projects that promise reasonable economic returns. Outreach processes may not avert all opposition, but the participants' investment of time and energy often wins effective support. Furthermore, community engagement processes demonstrate the developer's commitment as a responsible and responsive member of the community, concerned with making it a better place for all to live and work.

Over the years, ULI has published a number of books treating the art and science of engaging the community in planning for development. One of the earliest was *Working with the Community: A Developer's Guide,* published in 1985, followed in 1992 by Debra Stein's *Winning Community Support for Land Use Projects,* and in 1994 by *Pulling Together: A Planning and Development Consensus-Building Manual* (published in cooperation with several other organizations). The current volume marks the continuation of ULI's recognition of the necessity and power of engaging community groups in decisions about development. The book provides developers, planners, attorneys, and local residents with the latest tools and techniques for reaching out to community and neighborhood groups for input in the development process.

A decade or two ago, the concepts of multiday charrettes and organized sequences of public discussions about proposed projects, while not unknown, were relatively untried. Although public agencies increasingly were recognizing the value and political necessity of citizen participation in decision making about community development, developers were still inclined to go it alone. Typically, they marshalled consultant teams to tackle the task of gaining project approval with little, if any, involvement of local residents and community leaders.

However, developers' efforts to engage the community are growing more important, encouraged by two trends: the growing resistance of many communities to development projects that may introduce disturbing changes to the neighborhood, and the increasing interest of many residents and community leaders in the form and appearance of proposed projects. NIMBYism—Not in My Back Yard worries—stem from concerns about the effects of planned new developments on established areas. And communities interested in promoting the principles of smart growth are eager to encourage project designs that respond to those principles. Developers can alleviate both concerns through involving the community in the development process.

Citizens and public officials are learning more every day about the value of applying smart growth principles to improve community development. Principles such as encouraging development that will achieve compact, mixed-use, walkable urban and suburban environments will improve transportation and conserve open space. Smart growth also is about communities helping to widen the choices available to all residents for types of housing, living environments, and means of travel. Thus, an important smart growth principle deals with the "how" of making these choices. It urges inclusive public decision making that directly involves citizens in important determinations about the community's future development.

Most communities now expect to involve citizens in such discussions. Public officials and nonprofit organizations regularly organize processes to obtain serious citizen input on growth policies. As this book will show, developers can learn from this experience and use outreach processes to help tailor their development proposals to meet community needs while maintaining project feasibility—and to move more quickly through the permit process as well. This principle of smart growth is smart for both communities and developers.

This publication explains in plain terms why and how developers can undertake community engagement processes—how they work and the benefits they can achieve. It describes why, in these days of more complex projects and development approval procedures, it pays to win citizen support rather than fight opposition. It illustrates how collaborative approaches to project decision making can achieve positive ends. It also details how community engagement processes are organized and managed, including the formulation of a strategic plan, identification of key leaders and issues, the structuring of a process to win community acceptance, and descriptions of discussion and communication tools.

Seven case studies illustrate on-the-ground examples of various types of community engagement programs that have benefited developers and communities alike. The projects described in the studies range in character from small, 100-acre projects to large chunks of cities and counties; from mostly residential developments to mixed-use, resort, and transit-oriented developments; and from small-city and inner-city to greenfield areas. Lessons drawn from the case studies also highlight themes and concepts discussed in the main text.

—Douglas R. Porter

Contents

Part I Making Room at the Table: The Need for Community Engagement

The Overlooked Market for Development

Community engagement can be a lifeline for developers. Outreach processes can overcome project opposition that is often poorly informed and fearful of the unknown consequences of development. For local officials, they help create community support in circumstances fraught with political peril. For community residents, citizen engagement offers the chance to learn about the dynamics of development and the significance of public policies, and to contribute to designs of projects that will affect the quality of life of their community.

DOES THIS SCENARIO look familiar? Less than a year ago, a project development team was sitting around a conference table strewn with reports, maps, and drawings. The group was discussing next steps for initiating a transit-oriented, mixed-use development project to be built on a city infill site. The project had everything going for it: a strong market, positive feedback from potential financial partners, an attractive design concept, smart-growth features that pleased the city's planning department. The discussion focused, however, on a troubling obstacle: the thorny opposition of a politically connected neighborhood group. Members of the group were raising a ruckus about the project, causing planning commissioners to reconsider their tentative support. Until this organization's concerns could be assuaged, forward progress was at a standstill.

Oops! While the developer's project manager had covered all the bases in testing the project's market, financial readiness, and initial design concept, she had given less attention to the views of neighborhood leaders and residents. With the latest news, she realized that they essentially comprise another "market" for development projects, a market that needs to be engaged early in the planning phase for new development, lest a project get hijacked farther down the line.

The community's political leadership was equally concerned. The project promised to fulfill many of the smart growth principles that are guiding community development these days. It appeared to be in the right place, at the right time, with the right design. The trouble was that the local governmental leaders had not fully involved community residents in working out how smart growth principles would be applied in various neighborhoods. People had not had sufficient opportunity to learn what these principles meant and the benefits they might bring to the future development of the community. Lacking that knowledge, they recognized only the immediate effects of the project on their neighborhood. As if driving in a sudden fog on the highway, they slammed on the brakes.

Oops! While the developer's project manager had covered all the bases in testing the project's market, financial readiness, and initial design concept, she had given less attention to the views of neighborhood leaders and residents. With the latest news, she realized that they essentially comprise another "market" for development projects, a market that needs to be engaged early in the planning phase for new development, lest a project get hijacked farther down the line.

Staying Alive: The Vital Role of Community Engagement

Developers once relied on teams of consultants and lawyers to shepherd projects through approval, a "hands-off" tack increasingly unsuccessful in today's more complex environment. Direct engagement of the community from the start can go a long way toward addressing all parties' interests and concerns for a winning outcome.

AND REALLY, WHO COULD BLAME neighborhood residents for being skittish? Developers have been accustomed to employing attorneys and a roster of consultants to shepherd projects through the local approval process, reinforcing the divide between themselves and those whose interests they purportedly serve. Today, public perception of developers is decidedly more unfavorable than in the past. As more and more communities feel saddled with projects wholly unworthy of their affection, they seem unable—unwilling, even—to weed out the good from the bad. Neighbors await the bulldozer with trepidation, wondering whether the development will be an eyesore, whether it will force out small businesses, whether they will even be able to afford to live there anymore. Against a backdrop of growing animosity, developers, city planners, elected officials, and others involved in community growth have learned the hard way about the necessity of involving the wider community in guiding development and giving the go-ahead for specific development projects.

How the experts maneuver through such processes to a successful conclusion has been the subject of whole books (some listed in the reference section). Typically, the developer's team of consultants builds a compelling case for approval of the project and structures a carefully rehearsed presentation to the hearing board to highlight project benefits. Most times, the team's contacts with community leaders consist of one-on-one interviews to identify potential supporters of the project and define issues that need to be addressed. Community residents are given their only opportunity to speak about the issues at the scheduled public hearings, which can amount to a lame exercise in participatory democracy, the requisite public involvement that many citizens have come to view as a charade. Otherwise, the developer and his consultants are fully in charge of preparing the case, rounding up support, and providing the information necessary for officials to reach their desired outcome.

Yet this scenario is changing, prompted by rising levels of conflict in public decision making about community development. Developers have grown to respect the strength of opposition and its effects on project proposals. In many communities, contentious climates for development have grown out of the fears of residents over rampant traffic congestion, overcrowded schools, disappearing fields and forests, and other concerns. In some cases, residents' concerns are based on past history with developers who produced something other than they promised. Political decisions become more risky as controversies erupt over almost any project proposal, often fed by imprecise knowledge and outlandish assumptions. Even projects notable for their attention to civic consciousness, environmental sensitivity, and innovative design have been treated with a slash-and-burn mentality. Development that meets or surpasses all the regulatory requirements and might appear routinely approvable by local authorities can be thwarted almost overnight by opposition focused on seemingly narrow concerns. Such experiences repeatedly demonstrate that opponents' wielding of political pull, delaying tactics, and even lawsuits can turn a winning project into a loser.

Even projects notable for their attention to civic consciousness, environmental sensitivity, and innovative design have been treated with a slash-and-burn mentality. Development that meets or surpasses all the regulatory requirements and might appear routinely approvable by local authorities can be thwarted almost overnight by opposition focused on seemingly narrow concerns.

Much better is a process in which those involved in development genuinely engage the community in decision making about important aspects of the built environment. Community development, after all, is increasingly recognized as a joint public/private responsibility. (Smart growth principles build on that concept.) Theoretically, according to the old model, the private sector builds houses and shopping centers and other projects while the public sector provides quality standards and supports development with public facilities and services. In practice, of course, that conceptualization is overly simple. It omits consideration of projects that combine public and private investments and buildings, developers' increasing responsibility for funding and constructing many public facilities, and regulatory approaches that allow negotiated flexibility in meeting certain standards and requirements. Nowadays, cities and towns are built by a union of public and private efforts that demands a collaborative approach to decision making.

Nevertheless (or perhaps, as a result), securing public approvals of proposed policies and projects is much more complicated than in the past, and interrelationships between the public and private sectors are increasingly challenging. Land use, planning, and development issues have become more complex. The parties involved are not easily identified and may stretch across a wide spectrum of community interests. Public decisions on development proposals now often entail lengthy negotiations, difficult choices about community benefits and costs, and delicate weighing of off-setting effects. Decisions these days are seldom made by a close network of community leaders acting for the general public. Community officials and residents no longer automatically view development as beneficial, although individual property rights continue to be jealously guarded. State agencies and city councils often work at cross purposes—states promoting private property rights with city councils seeking greater regulation.

In addition, public regulations have become more detailed, complex, and all-encompassing. Guiding documents such as comprehensive plans often are presented in hundreds of pages, and zoning ordinances specify elaborate rules for features such as landscaping, signs, parking, and communication towers in addition to permitted land uses. Developers are frequently confronted with requests for design changes and additional project features that may add to development costs and require detailed studies of potential effects on a project's marketability and its financial foundation.

Projects have grown in complexity as well, by mixing a variety of uses, experimenting with new site and building designs, revamping historic buildings, and finding ways to retain wetlands and other environmental features within developed areas. As market demands for the products of development have expanded and diffused into dozens of niche markets, developers have innovated and expanded the variety of building forms and settings they plan to construct.

Much of this flexibility comes as a direct response to the principles of smart growth, a concept strongly supported by professional and special interest groups but, not surprisingly, less well known by the general public. Smart growth principles are much in the news for those in the know, calling for more attention to developing compact, mixed-use, pedestrian-friendly, architecturally distinctive communities that offer transportation choices and conserve open space—a major challenge to past practices of community development, but one that appears to take advantage of changing demographic trends across the nation.

In theory, who could object to such enlightened views of community building and growth? These concepts are increasingly viewed by players on the inside as beneficial goals for future development, applicable in newly developing areas as well as existing cities and towns. Advocacy groups have sprung up across the nation and in many commu-

Today, public perception of developers is decidedly more unfavorable than in the past.

THE BIG PICTURE: STEPPING UP ADVOCACY

One of the main obstacles to achieving sound development is the lack of knowledge concerning sound practices. For a variety of reasons, the general public's design literacy is astonishingly low. Developers, architects, planners, activists, and others involved in the building professions should bear some of the responsibility for educating others about the principles of smart growth—what they are, why they are necessary, why they work best for all of us over the long term. By serving as a resource for others, whether by volunteering to speak at schools and community centers, or by getting involved in educational programming and lobbying for the inclusion of design-related subjects in the mainstream curriculum, those in the professions can vastly improve the chances of achieving high-quality, well-received development.

The smart growth design of Hellgate Meadows in Missoula, Montana, which clustered attractively designed homes close to each other and to nearby services, has found ready acceptance in the marketplace.

Consider this: If children can glean the interrelatedness of all living things in an elementary school science class, can this interrelatedness not be further elucidated by teaching them the principles of smart growth? Far from being dry and theoretical, or idealistic and abstract, these principles speak to the very concrete ways in which people live, work, and play, to the ways in which we interact on a daily basis with the world around us. To speak of community growth and development in these terms is to recognize the intricate, interdependent web underlying the concept of smart growth. The principles are worth repeating:

- To pursue *sustainable development* that challenges communities to seek to develop in ways that will advance and integrate environmental conservation, economic growth, and social equity;
- To employ techniques for constructing *"green" buildings* that decrease energy consumption, reduce rainwater runoff, and use renewable or recycled materials;

This image of a picturesque commercial street in Athens, Georgia, was used in the North St. Lucie charrette to provide a real-world example of an attractive form of development that reflects smart growth principles.

- To create *neighborhood designs* that encourage social and economic interaction, provide visually pleasurable and human-scale spaces and building groups, and reduce land consumption;
- To plan *town centers and activity centers* that cluster retail, business, and residential uses in walkable environments;
- To have development oriented to multimodal travel networks such as intensive *developments around transit stations* and extensive *walking and biking pathway systems;*
- To provide for community and regional design of *green infrastructure systems* of parks, recreation facilities, and environmentally sensitive areas connected by trails and greenways into the urban fabric of developing areas.[1]

nities to encourage consideration of these forms of development by developers and public officials. Yet in reality, development policies and regulations in many communities pose obstacles for applying these innovative ideas. Neighbors of projects that propose to heighten density and bring new uses to the area, for example, often generate resident opposition, and that opposition has grown increasingly sophisticated in its methods. Project opponents have learned the effective use of such legal and political tools as referendum petitions and email campaigns to affect decisions. These methods demand a new approach.

Early outreach and community participation in consideration of proposed development can no longer be viewed as a softball stratagem. For developers and for communities, the benefits of achieving cooperation far outweigh the costs of unwilling compromises reached through confrontation and controversy. When community engagement is mishandled, so-called "victories" by one side or the other usually lead to losses for everyone. Developers lose time, money, and regard for the predictability of the process. Local officials lose the public trust and credibility with the private sector. In raising development costs and sapping energy, lengthy disputes represent disinvestments in communities and society as a whole. Alternatively, through community engagement, developers and representatives of public interests can focus their energies on achieving a fair and predictable quality of development, rather than spending time counter-punching each other. The community at large can gain confidence that its input will be taken seriously and that development projects will contribute to a more livable community.

UNDERSTANDING CITIZEN CONCERNS

Communities are complicated places. It's not that people are necessarily opposed to change. More often, residents of a community undergoing growth and development are simply afraid, and their fear can arise from not seeing the full picture. Misunderstandings about the dynamics of community change, misconceptions of proposed projects, and bewilderment about the unknown effects of development generate not only fear of the unknown, but also possibly about known project qualities whose effects can be alleviated if understood early in the approval process.

Fears often relate to projected increases in population and activities—more traffic, school overcrowding, resident displacement, rising demands on parks and community centers and police services. Some stem from perceptions of a building's visual appearance. Citizens might also be uneasy about how new people will fit into the neighborhood.

Such concerns can be exaggerated, especially if residents are generally distrustful of the capabilities of local governments to deal with growth problems, or of the motivations of developers to build projects distinguished by their enduring value to the community, and not merely by their profitability to their developers and investors. The guardedness, disillusion, and cynicism in evidence will not be put to rest by standard procedures that call for a public hearing or two. Citizens know that such hearings typically offer few opportunities for understanding the real effects of proposed developments, and almost no chance for reasonable discourse about the pros and cons of a proposed project.

All of these suspicions can prove to be unstated but powerful influences on citizen attitudes toward new development. The antidote proposed by this book is to open up opportunities for citizens to learn about proposed projects and thus contribute to decisions on project plans and designs. The book's premise is that when people are well informed about community development in general, and proposed projects in particular, the likelihood of securing their support for a project greatly increases.

Tailoring Approaches for Community Engagement

Whether employed to address long-range or immediate concerns, community engagement processes come in all shapes and sizes. But their defining characteristic is collaboration—recognizing, respecting, and working with the powerful players, the influential advisers, and the citizens directly affected.

THIS BOOK USES THE TERM "COMMUNITY engagement" to encompass a constellation of efforts to engage the attention, input, and ultimate support of community residents for improving the quality of community development. Public officials and agencies increasingly seek such community participation in decision making about growth and change. But this book focuses particularly on how developers can sponsor and participate in outreach activities to help shape their projects to meet community-friendly goals. Whether undertaken by public agencies or by developers, community engagement processes tend to use similar techniques for involving and learning from participants. The process seeks participation of individual residents and businesses, interest groups of all kinds, and public officials in consideration of—and, hopefully, agreement on—development policies and project proposals.

Past approaches reflect mindsets that tend to favor decision making by a chosen few who make plans behind closed doors. By contrast, community engagement seeks to establish a collaborative approach to problem solving among all the interests in community development. Developers, notes Michael Thomsett in his book on combating NIMBYism, are not always visionaries, but their struggle to work with members of the community rather than in conflict with them is invariably desirable.[2] The power of collaborative processes emanates from inclusion of and respect for the variety of affected interests, whether they are the ultimate decision makers, or influential advisers to decision makers, or the people affected by the decisions.

Many communities now routinely employ outreach and participation processes to involve citizens in public planning and policy initiatives. Public officials may wish to establish a broad base of community support for a long-range plan or a comprehensive revision of a zoning ordinance. The North St. Lucie County (Florida) community engagement process was structured to reach agreement on broad policies to guide future development and is being followed up by more detailed planning for implementation. Such long-range planning by public agencies often involves complex concepts, large quantities of information, and multiyear commitments by participants who must understand and finally agree on policies and regulations. The process may reach out to thousands of residents. It may require a series of midpoint products along the way, such as formulation of a community vision and determination of basic policies to guide community development. Frequently, it will end with a formal adoption by elected officials of a vision statement, a plan, or an ordinance. No small affair, this type of process absorbs immense amounts of time and energy by local officials, but generates a new clarity about the direction of future community development.

The North St. Lucie County process involved over 350 participants in a seven-day charrette. It required weeks of research and organization by consultants and, following the charrette, numerous technical discussions with county staff to reach a conclusion. Even then, the process was just an important stepping-stone to more detailed work for the creation of a comprehensive plan and implementation of regulations for development.

In contrast, the developer involved in a 40-acre project in Missoula, Montana, elected to sponsor a public meeting and four-day design charrette to broaden public acceptance of a neotraditional project he had already sketched out. The process allowed him to test public reception to the innovative design, resolve some issues with neighboring property owners, secure solid support for project approval, and quickly move forward on development once the project permit was obtained.

Development issues stir intensive discussions among participants in well-organized public meetings, such as this one in North St. Lucie County.

Community engagement processes take many forms. They can involve an elaborate sequence of research, events, and media communications over months and years, or a few meetings with interested parties to work out details of a project or policy. Preparation for meetings can benefit from the involvement of specialists in discussion facilitation, visualization of design options, and many other techniques for presenting and interactively discussing information and ideas. The efforts can be assisted by in-house staff and/or one or an array of consulting firms. Organizers of engagement processes will work with community groups, local officials, and developers to shape the scope and character of outreach efforts to consider potential community impacts of proposed policies and projects.

As discussed in detail in the following sections, community engagement processes can employ a variety of techniques and tools for describing the character and potential impacts of the policies or projects, for organizing and conducting discussions in many types of venues and formats, and for communicating ideas and decisions through formal and informal mediums.

Types of Engagement Processes

"What'll It Be?" Pick and choose, mix and match among engagement processes that can serve to address and clarify, negotiate and resolve, detail and implement. The menu of options features:

- **Consensus Building**
- **Dispute or Conflict Resolution**
- **Mediation**
- **Conciliation**
- **Facilitation.**

THE TERM "COMMUNITY ENGAGEMENT process" refers to a variety of specific methods for achieving agreement about community development policies and projects. A similar general term is "collaborative process." Both suggest that participants work cooperatively to reach some degree of consensus on policies affecting development and desirable components of specific projects. Professionals involved in resolving issues that have stirred controversies over community development use a variety of terms and approaches that are somewhat similar but organized to elicit various degrees of agreement and ratification. The type of agreement, however, and the means by which it is reached, may vary according to the methods employed.

Consensus building takes a broadly inclusive group having diverse views and, through discussion, brings them to general consent about a development approach or plan. Assent to individual aspects of policies or projects in this case tends to be subordinated to the acceptance of the bundle of characteristics (the specific plan or set of policies) for which adequate compromises have been discussed and agreed upon. It is often an advisory process that ends by reporting findings and conclusions to an official body for a final decision.

Dispute or conflict resolution sets the stage for direct discussions between two (and sometimes more) defined parties to resolve their conflicts over one or more specific issues. While solutions may be invented during discussions to win agreement from the antagonists, the process tends to accept that some aspects of the dispute are "either-or" issues for which tradeoffs or compromises must be negotiated. The end product is usually documented in a written agreement.

Mediation involves a mediator directing negotiation between conflicting parties to reach a reconciliation or settlement of issues, often cemented with a legal agreement. As used in labor relations, mediation usually begins with firm but conflicting views of two parties. Mediators help keep the focus on specific issues, requiring an informed leader who takes a direct interest in finding points of reconciliation. Arbitration can be viewed as a variant of mediation in which the arbitrator, after hearing from and discussing the parties' points of view, decides the outcome. The ultimate arbitration process, of course, is a lawsuit.

Giving Is Receiving: Developers as Participants

Participating in community planning meetings gives developers a foot in the door. Not only will showing up to hear the citizens' side of the story be illuminating, but it gives developers a chance to meet the public and share with it their own perspective. It may seem time-consuming, but it is well worth the effort.

PARTICIPATION IN PUBLICLY SPONSORED discussions about the ways their communities are developing—aside from their particular projects—can be beneficial for both developers and the community. Developers signal their acceptance of a role as responsible citizens of the community by their visible presence and participation in discussions about long-term development goals and policies. In addition, the opportunities for developers' input on development issues can contribute useful information and perspectives about community concerns such as affordable housing and downtown development. A more direct benefit is getting to know the people who regularly participate in community discussions about development and whose opinions will affect the outcomes of such discussions. Understanding, if not agreeing with, their point of view can be helpful in future negotiations over project approval policy and regulatory issues. Developers located on the scene may have an advantage in access to local community leaders, while development firms whose activity is scattered among many communities may need to establish associations with local firms or consultants to get a footing.

One benefit to developers of participating in planning and visioning exercises is that it can deepen their understanding of

Conciliation usually aims to stage individual meetings with parties that have a history of conflict and are unwilling to enter into an open discussion process. A conciliator works to help them better understand the issues at stake, the nature of a proposed discussion process, and the benefits of participation. A conciliation process stresses recognition of a mutuality of concerns and interests across group lines.

Facilitation is a discussion process coached by a trained leader that engages participants in thinking through issues and conflicts to reach a degree of agreement. (Facilitation methods are used in most of the processes described above.) Usually, facilitators assist large- and small-group discussions by clarifying the issues, eliciting views and concerns, and leading a group to achieving some degree of consensus on a course of action.

the story behind adopted policies and regulations—the basic concerns that have been driving the political process and its decisions about the form, location, and design of development. In effect, they are participating in creating the policy and regulatory framework they will have to live with as they continue to develop projects.

And what of developers and business leaders who find that a lengthy series of planning discussions absorbs too much of their workday? They appear infrequently, frustrating their intentions and those of process organizers who wish to attract the widest possible community participation. Short of devoting an unreasonable amount of time to outreach, ways can be found to assure continued participation. For example, their views could be represented by staff of development organizations such as the local homebuilder's group. Or they could be scheduled to participate in focus groups or other limited-agenda discussions, or to be involved at key points in the process. Still, any of these alternatives requires that developers do their homework in reading newsletters and memoranda summarizing the results of meetings they miss. Those weary of attending what seems to be an endless series of meetings should remind themselves of the perils of avoidance: such community discussions often lead to policy and regulatory decisions that that will shape, make, or break future development.

Another lesson developers can learn from engaging in community planning meetings is that the same tools and techniques used in gaining agreement to a local government's comprehensive plan can be applied to generating support for a private development. Developers can and do sponsor community engagement processes. The process undertaken to reach agreement on California's Pleasant Hill BART Station plan is an example. Although BART and the three communities around the station needed a plan to guide redevelopment, the chief beneficiary of the charrette process undertaken at Pleasant Hill was Millennium Partners, the developer selected to build the project. The Hellgate Meadows charrette in Missoula, Montana, was sponsored by the developer to help familiarize the community about traditional neighborhood design and to air issues about relationships and access to adjoining properties in a neutral setting. He was prepared to let community leaders have a hand in working out reasonable solutions.

...the same tools and techniques used in gaining agreement to a local government's comprehensive plan can be applied to generating support for a private development.

Consultants: Enough Bang for the Buck?

Consultants who know the local scene and have experience using the tools and techniques of community engagement can be a developer's ace in the hole. They can be employed in all areas of the process, for different durations, at many budgets. Their expertise and assistance have proved invaluable in tackling misinformation, creating and managing productive work teams, identifying and defining workable solutions, and ultimately, achieving project approval.

DEVELOPERS EMPLOY CONSULTANTS all the time. Development firms, whether they have large or small staffs, tend to form teams of consultants to conduct most of the detailed work associated with obtaining project approvals and construction design. They do this because they need specialists in planning, design, engineering, and other aspects of development and, just as important, they need professionals who are knowledgeable about local planning and regulatory processes, local political issues, and the local leadership structure. As site and building design have become more important in gaining project approval, firms specializing in innovative architectural and planning design have gained prominence. Transportation and market research consultants are often part of the team. Also, specialists in organizing and managing public meetings, charrettes, visioning processes, and other forms of community involvement are increasingly in demand as community participation in development planning has become more widely used.

Consultants based in communities outside a project's location can bring valuable perspectives to the table. Often they have seen and participated in projects that have run afoul of local policies or interest groups, and have gained experience in dealing with the conflicts that emerged. In addition, they can bring a fresh view to the issues and point out courses of action that can lead to a resolution. When the Park City ski resort project was threatened by a group petitioning for a referendum, the out-of-town consultant conducted an opinion poll. It determined that many local residents actually were potential supporters of the project. The consultant's suggestions for capitalizing on the developer's long-term relationships within the community helped generate a support group that overcame opposition.

Most consultant teams formed for the case study projects profiled in this book have been led by design and planning firms with considerable experience in formulating and managing community engagement processes. The lead consultants have brought other firms into the consultant team to add specialized knowledge, including architects skilled in the specific types of development contemplated for the project, designers capable of employing computer-aided visualization techniques, civil and transportation engineering firms, specialists in environmental concerns, and, if not otherwise provided by the lead firm, consultants trained in facilitation and public relations. Local firms are often added to the team to provide insights into local regulatory, leadership, and political aspects of the project. These groups of consultants are useful not only in providing a broad range of skills and experience, but also for supplying the manpower needed to staff the intensive public events that typically run on short deadlines.

Some may still question whether the benefits are worth the cost of employing consultants to mount community engagement campaigns. The case studies describe engagement processes that extend over two or three months, or up to a year or more for some large projects. Charrettes and other sequences of public discussions tend to be labor-intensive for the duration of the events. Bob Brugh in Missoula spent almost $100,000 for a four-day charrette and the subsequent plan and report preparation, not counting his own time. Brugh says that the work completed during that process allowed him to move directly into engineering specifications for subdivi-

...consultants are useful not only in providing a broad range of skills and experience, but also for supplying the manpower needed to staff the intensive public events that typically run on short deadlines.

Using quick sketches to stimulate discussion, consultants offer ideas for consideration by charrette participants. Here, the possibilities offered by one design for the Pleasant Hill station area are pointed out by the consultant staff.

sion development. RTKL's consulting team for the Rolling Mill Hill project in Nashville required a budget of about $135,000 for work with local officials and neighborhood residents over a period of six months or so. The resulting recommendations for building sites and uses made it possible for the redevelopment agency to immediately request developer proposals for construction on key sites.

The much larger and more complex planning process in Eastern Cambridge took almost a year and was budgeted at about $500,000. David Dixon of Goody Clancy in Boston, who led the effort, notes that the budget allowed for a battery of specialized consultants in transportation, market research, environmental issues, zoning, and other areas, in addition to the firm's designers assigned to the project. But, he reasons, for a project that will generate 12 million square feet of new construction worth at least a half billion dollars, a half million in consultant costs seems quite reasonable. The process not only firmed up a politically and technically feasible plan, but also documented recommendations for design guidelines pertaining to building uses, scale, and character, and generated a list of implementing actions including transportation, open space, and other improvements in the public realm. The fact that development began almost immediately after ratification of the plan indicates the extent to which the planning process laid a strong foundation for development.

In short, the consultant teams chosen for community engagement processes can be authorized to deliver not just community acceptance of a plan, but detailed designs and guidelines to enable rapid progress toward actual development. Developers interviewed for the case studies believed that the results were well worth the costs involved.

CHECKLIST

✓ Consider community engagement as a way of overcoming opposition that actually improves the project.

✓ All engagement processes are different, but no matter it will be necessary to work collaboratively and devote substantial time to the effort.

✓ Begin thinking about the menu of engagement options and how to employ consultants.

✓ Directly engage the community from the start to address all parties' interests and concerns.

Part II Crafting a Strategy for Community Engagement

Homing In on the Approach

Before you know what type of process you'll need, the following three questions need to be considered: What outcome am I looking for? What issues might arise from site conditions and the project's possible impacts on the area? Who are the people who need to be involved? The answers will establish the framework of the outreach effort.

A COMMUNITY ENGAGEMENT PROCESS is like grand opera. It deals with complicated and intriguing interpersonal relationships; it highlights proud divas such as elected officials and outspoken civic leaders; it ushers in a bickering chorus of believers and nonbelievers; its scenes are draped with grandiose design plans and studies galore; it is beautifully choreographed to sweep multitudes on and off the stage at a moment's notice; and it is long . . . very long. (Even four-day charrettes require weeks of preparation and months of follow-up technical work.) Now imagine the opera producer, who selects the divas and orchestra conductor, works out the roster of singers and dancers, and chooses the set designer and the choreographer. He or she also schedules rehearsals and directs the stagehands who work behind the curtain to set up the next act. Operas—and community engagement processes—*are complicated.*

As in an opera production, all the activities and commotion generated by a process of community engagement demand advance planning. In order to select the most effective tools and techniques to use in such a process, its organizers must take into account (1) the nature of the final product desired at the end of the process; (2) the issues that may be raised by site conditions and potential project impacts on the surrounding area; and (3) the identity and roles of the cast of characters who need to be involved. The results of these efforts will establish the basic concerns to be addressed by the outreach process.

Developers who have carried out previous projects in a community will have acquired much of this information already. And developers who have done their homework in the process of tracking market opportunities and identifying and acquiring or optioning a site will have become somewhat familiar with conditions around the site, the general character of the community, and its regulatory posture toward similar projects.

However, even for those with some knowledge of local outlooks on development, it is important at this preparatory stage to obtain a first-hand picture of the project locale and its potential reception by the surrounding neighborhood and the community as a whole. This need not require a highly detailed survey; rather, it can take the form of a brief but intensive reconnaissance to size up the odds concerning the proposed project. The three areas of interest—identification of the desired end product, critical issues in community development, and key community leaders—are likely to be investigated more or less concurrently.

The three areas of interest—identification of the desired end product, critical issues in community development, and key community leaders—are likely to be investigated more or less concurrently.

Opportunities remain to be identified for adaptive use of the historic but rather plain-Jane car barns in the Rolling Mill Hill redevelopment area.

Frame the Desired Outcome: Begin at the End

Desirable outcomes from outreach programs can run the gamut from formal agreements reached with one or more key organizations, to majority consent among the members of an official or semiofficial advisory group, to a general understanding and acceptance of the proposal by participants in the process. Sometimes it is enough simply to establish positive feelings among people affected by a proposal, especially if they can be counted on to publicly support it.

THE STARTING POINT FOR ANY community engagement process is defining the desired end product—in this case, the outcome that will be considered satisfactory for the developer. City planning agencies frequently engage in citizen participation exercises to establish a guiding "vision" for the community, or to test the popularity of certain strategies and policies, or to build broad community support for future ratifications of plans and regulations. Although planners may have a professional interest in the quality of the end product of such a process, they are not necessarily looking for closure in this phase of plan development. Rather, they are hoping to arrive at some level of agreement about palatable policies or action programs that might be adopted in the future. The North St. Lucie County process, for example, was but a prelude to more detailed studies and plans.

By contrast, developers know they intend to obtain community support for a specific project designed with features consciously chosen to respond to market demands, site conditions, architectural concepts, and other factors that will ensure their potential success in the marketplace. The developers' interest is in winning approval for a carefully crafted development proposal rather than a policy position that leaves room for several outcomes and might or might not be implemented. Developers usually have relatively little "give" in their projects that could allow radical changes in planned uses or sharp reductions in allowable densities. They are engaging the community to obtain its acceptance that the projects as planned will satisfy important public or neighborhood interests—and perhaps add significant value—while avoiding undue impacts on their surroundings. While developers may accept suggestions for modest improvements that will improve a plan's chances of obtaining official approval, it is critical for them to fashion a community participation program that will generate positive responses. They don't want to run the risk of sparking negative reactions that will stop a project in its tracks.

Bob Brugh in Missoula was concerned with obtaining support for a specific design concept and working out some sensitive issues regarding relationships between the proposed development and adjoining properties. The general support the project received was icing on the cake. McCormack Baron Salazar had to overcome the long-term suspicions of Crawford Square residents that development meant resident displacement. Both development firms worked to create an atmosphere of collaborative problem solving and trust rather than structure an up-or-down vote on a plan.

For most developers, the outreach focus can be framed in this way:

- Recognizing that 100 percent agreement on a proposed project is impossible, given the disparate interests involved, what extent of consensus will provide a response to the issues that will satisfy the community's decision makers?
- How can such an agreement be expressed or documented? For complex, multiphase projects, developers may need to reach out to the community to establish a broad base of support. The process may require a carefully structured series of community participation events and special attention to graphic displays. The support may be expressed by the general consent of participants in a publicized plan or a documented vote by a community task force set up to advise elected officials.

While developers may accept suggestions for modest improvements that will improve a plan's chances of obtaining official approval, it is critical for them to fashion a community participation program that will generate positive responses.

The Eastern Cambridge planning study followed this course. Although not directed by developers, the study was established to create the planning framework that would allow developers to move quickly to specific project proposals. The study committee acted as the centrum of decision making for the plan. It took into account the ideas of charrette participants and the consultant team in making recommendations for a plan and implementation program to the city council. The advisory committee agreed on a plan despite dissent from one charrette participant, who insisted to the end that the plan provided for too little open space. While that lone participant may have spoken the truth, the committee decided that the majority supported the plan as presented.

For projects located in areas prone to development disputes, developers may focus on one-on-one discussions with community leaders and meetings with predefined interest groups to identify and resolve community concerns and issues. The end product in this case might be supportive testimony by community representatives at public hearings. The Park City case study illustrates such a scenario, which involved the developer in organizing a prodevelopment group whose advocacy could win public support for the project. Or a developer of a small project may negotiate with neighborhood leaders to alleviate possible project impacts and to help satisfy specific neighborhood needs, with the agreement coming in the form of lack of opposition.

The Pleasant Hill community engagement process aimed toward establishing positive attitudes about the project among members of participating interest groups, which had been intensively concerned with the project for years. Interim decisions were checked with the key clients—BART, the county, and the developer—before they were finalized. The resulting plan was then ratified through implementing agreements among the three clients.

Evaluate Site Conditions and Potential Project Impacts

Hit the streets to learn about a neighborhood's past, people-watch, find out what residents like and don't like about living there, and see how your project will fit in. At this point developers and their consultants will also need to supplement these important, yet informal findings with solid data describing site and area conditions and potential issues that might be raised by the proposed development.

MOST CONCERNS ABOUT PROJECTS will arise from site conditions and potential impacts on adjoining uses, which argues for an intensive scrutiny of the site and its surroundings. Developers like to get their feet on the ground, and walking the site and driving around the neighborhood, in addition to assembling available information, will provide a valuable perspective on potential issues and opportunities. Some may be generated by the site's physical conditions and others by the project's potential impacts—positive and negative—that will affect its acceptance by the neighborhood. The need for good local knowledge cannot be overstated.

The Neighborhood Setting

The analysis begins with focusing on the neighborhood setting for the future project and the conditions of the site itself, including the following aspects:

- The prevailing character of buildings and uses in the area surrounding the site—and how they got that way. Learn something about the history of the place and how it has changed over time. Observe the kinds of people who live or work there. (Information about the character of the area, its residents and workers, and its status within the community is often readily available from local planning or economic development offices, the newspapers, or census reports).
- Aspects of the site that currently affect neighborhood residents—features they enjoy such as schools, parks, proximity to pleasant meadows or woodlands; or conditions that they may wish to improve, such as traffic patterns or over-grown or unsightly conditions.
- Landscape and environmental features which, if preserved, will demonstrate the developer's concerns for high-quality development (and perhaps add to its market value).
- How the proposed project will fit into the neighborhood. What features, now missing, could contribute to neighborhood livability, such as on-site amenities or connections to other neighborhoods? What aspects of the project could stir concerns—buildings looming over existing homes, for example, or generating traffic onto neighborhood streets, or children in new homes overcrowding the local schools?
- Project qualities that can contribute to meeting community goals and policies, as articulated in local comprehensive plans and by statements of advocacy groups.

The Crawford Square neighborhood had been decimated by previous urban renewal activities on the site but represented a key redevelopment opportunity next to downtown Pittsburgh.

CAUTIONS TO CONSIDER IN SITE ASSESSMENT

Huddle with the city's planning staff to understand the project approval process—what approvals are needed, who makes the decisions, and what discretion is available. See how the project conforms to the jurisdiction's comprehensive or general plan policies and zoning requirements. If it measures up in all respects, the project may have smooth sailing for obtaining approval. Chances are, though, that some project features run contrary to one or more plan policies or regulatory provisions, or that a so-called "discretionary" review process with extra conditions and hearings is necessary to accomplish the kind of project being proposed. Either of these occurrences opens up opportunities for opposition based on new issues, as indicated below.

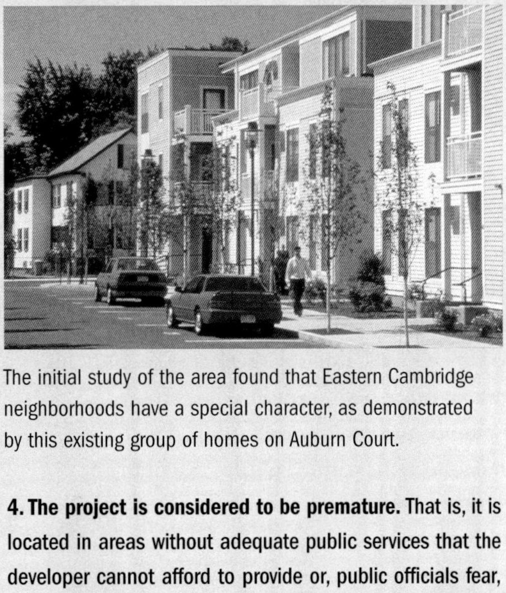

The initial study of the area found that Eastern Cambridge neighborhoods have a special character, as demonstrated by this existing group of homes on Auburn Court.

1. Why is the site available? Check the property's history to see whether it has been the subject of previous development proposals that have been shot down by opponents. If the issues raised at the time remain controversial, they will have to be addressed.

2. Is this a good project in the wrong place? Local citizens may view the project as simply out of character for the community or neighborhood—too large, too dense, too much surface parking, too modern in design—in short, too unlike the present community.

3. The project may compete with existing development that residents hold dear. This is especially significant if the existing development—a historic downtown, for example—is having trouble maintaining its economic life and the proposed project—a big-box retail store, for example—represents major competition.

4. The project is considered to be premature. That is, it is located in areas without adequate public services that the developer cannot afford to provide or, public officials fear, that will induce other development that is undesirable at this time. Public timing of readiness for development is becoming as important as private timing for the market.

5. The project may fall between the cracks if it requires plan or zoning changes, or if either the plan or ordinances needs to be updated. In either case it may be years before the dust settles enough for project approval.

Goody Clancy, after evaluating site conditions in Eastern Cambridge, realized that the issues raised by residents did not necessarily jibe with neighborhood conditions and identifiable development opportunities. That called for an educational process to provide information that might alter residents' perceptions to conform with reality. Therefore, the first meetings with the advisory committee were organized to provide opportunities for learning about traffic conditions (most traffic was going through the neighborhood rather than generated within it), density considerations (higher-density development in selected locations might improve walkability), and park spaces (smaller was often better). The consultants also were able to point out that substantial vacant land in the North Point area could allow well-designed development that would enhance the neighborhood. The initial neighborhood analysis provided a good jumping-off point for engaging the community.

Partners and project managers at McCormack Baron Salazar have made a point of "walking the territory" when they initiate projects, which are often in cities the firm has not worked in previously. Tony Salazar describes how his partner Richard Baron will walk along the streets to identify historic or other significant buildings that should be preserved, street and pedestrian connections with adjoining neighborhoods, existing shops and services, and the civic heart of the area. At the same time, he is observing residents and street life to sense the social character of the area. This early sense for how the neighborhood functions is an invaluable aid to subsequent planning.

Research and Evaluation Tools

Aside from site visits and digging up some basic information on the area, developers and their consultants will need to prepare solid data to describe site and area conditions and potential issues that might be raised by the proposed development. Specialized consultants usually are employed to prepare these types of studies. In their preparation for public meetings, charrettes, and other public events, they will need to assemble information on the following aspects of the project and its possible benefits and impacts:

- Neighborhood design factors such as architectural qualities of existing and historic buildings, street patterns and connections, pleasurable views, and public facilities;
- Transportation analyses identifying major travel flows, congestion points, pedestrian and bicycle pathways, transit service, and projected changes in these characteristics given planned projects;

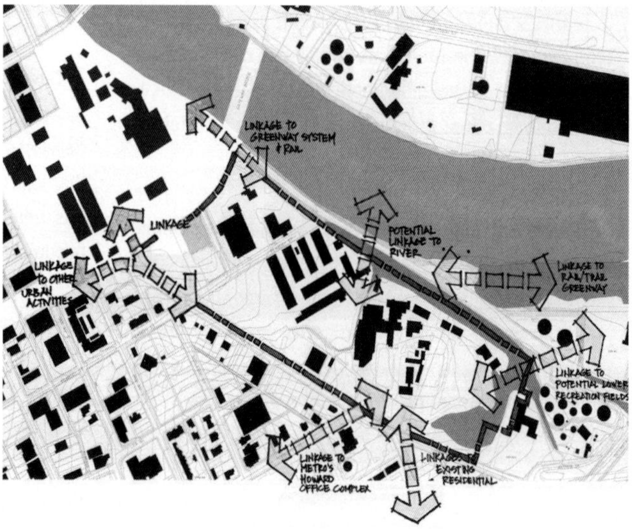

The design analysis pointed out opportunities to capitalize on existing linkages between the Rolling Mill Hill site and the surrounding area, including access to and along the river.

- Economic and market conditions and trends for the region, community, and site area, including household size and income variations, for each type of use planned for the proposed project;
- Projected fiscal benefits and impacts of the proposed project on city revenues and expenditures; and
- Environmental concerns and opportunities offered by the existing natural qualities of the site and area.

Some research tools can be used to evaluate specific aspects of interest. For example, transportation studies frequently include computer modeling of existing and proposed travel networks to enable projections of the potential effects of proposed development on travel patterns. One could benefit from learning about the variables that affect the outputs of such modeling efforts, as well as about the outputs themselves.

Such computer models and other software tools are regularly employed by consulting firms that work on real estate projects. Consultants acquire or develop software packages that assist them in making detailed studies of potential project impacts, including (in addition to transportation) environmental and fiscal impacts, effects on economic development and social equity, real estate market trends, and other aspects of community development. In addition, for use in planning future development, many local and regional government agencies own computer models that provide an abundance of detailed data relating to development trends and impacts.

Know the Parties at Interest

Public officials, administrative staff members, planning commissioners, business leaders, community activists, representatives of special-interest groups, former longtime elected officials, neighborhood leaders, residents, and employees in the area surrounding the proposed development constitute a group of stakeholders whose views should be sounded out.

RESIDENTS ARE MORE AWARE than ever of plans by "outsiders" to develop their communities. With real estate prices skyrocketing across the nation, working people being priced out of once affordable neighborhoods, and the growing pressure for housing across all levels of the economic spectrum, it doesn't take much to figure out that a weedy parking lot or dilapidated block might soon become . . . something else. It is the perceived threat of that something else that concerns us here, for residents almost always have a greater sense of what they *don't* want, rather than what they do. It is critical for developers to recognize the distinctive character of the community for which a project is slated. An initial assessment of what might be termed the "community clientele" will help in building a compelling case for the project. The parties to watch closely are those who will make or influence the decision to approve the project: the individuals or groups who have decision making authority, those who have formal or informal powers to support or block a decision, and those directly affected by a decision who may voice their opinions to the decision makers. Additional parties may be identified who are not directly affected by a proposed project but can be consulted for significant input on tangential issues.

Project developers should actually know these peoples' names and specific concerns, rather than simply make a list of possible outreach participants. Success in organizing community engagement depends on bringing the right interests into the process at the right time, and into any agreement that will emanate from the discussions. This will involve some hard work and take time at the start of the process, unless the developer or members of his development team have laid the groundwork during years of prior contacts and information gathering. Even then, if the project incorporates a different mix of uses than past ones or is located in an unfamiliar neighborhood, it will be necessary to expand the range of contacts and knowledge about local concerns and issues.

Success in organizing community engagement depends on bringing the right interests into the process at the right time, and into any agreement that will emanate from the discussions.

When working with the parties at interest, it helps to know something about their so-called "power base," internal structure, and relationships with other interest groups. Interest groups will exercise their influence to gain what they consider important goals that benefit their members. Interest group leaders can try to block decisions or escalate conflict to retain the allegiance of their members, but are often willing to negotiate mutually advantageous deals with other groups. They can be important players in making decisions depending on the strength of their power base and the personal character of their leaders. Private-sector organizations, in particular, are often structured so as to vest decision making power at the top, so that leaders of such groups can wield considerable power. Many citizen and nonprofit groups, however, tend to be less hierarchical and their leaders often must consult with group members before committing to a decision. Obtaining solid commitments on courses of action by representatives of this mix of groups can test the skills—and patience—of facilitators.

The Decision Makers

Development projects receive official permits through various procedures, depending on the jurisdiction's regulatory and administrative structure. But the permitting process often involves the legislative council of the city or county, staffs of the planning and related offices, and the planning commission. Usually the buck stops at the local council for projects that need comprehensive plan amendments, rezoning, and special exceptions. Frequently, the council must approve final subdivision plans. In their role as representatives of the entire community, these public officials may have the most comprehensive view of the social and economic impacts of growth and development. They most certainly have an interest in the political ramifications of negative impacts. And they usually understand the importance of development to the community's image held by outsiders. They know that high-quality projects can be sources of civic pride and promote a positive image of the community in the region and beyond.

Certainly the city council members in Nashville and Cambridge understood the political sensitivities inherent in initiating redevelopment projects in and around existing neighborhoods. The Rolling Mill Hill district in Nashville was not only a blight on the downtown area, but the city held significant and potentially valuable properties there. The central issue was clear: how to leverage the city's ownership to correct the blighted conditions. At the same time, however, the community engagement process had to balance citywide and neighborhood interests while coming up with a market-feasible development plan that would complement rather than compete with downtown activities.

Organizers of the North St. Lucie County charrette made sure to involve county officials such as Commissioner Doug Coward in the discussion process. (Charrette team leader Marcela Camblor stands on his right.)

As another example, city officials formulated the Eastern Cambridge planning study as a means of improving the living environment of several existing neighborhoods, but also to promote office, research, and retail activities that would increase the city's tax base—two conceivably opposing goals. The planning area included two major areas that offered attractive opportunities for substantial expansions of the city's employment base: the mostly vacant North Point industrial area, and the Kendall Square area already developed with offices and research facilities that could be enlarged and intensified. For city officials and community leaders, finding ways to encourage mixed-use development in these areas while supporting neighborhood revitalization was the central task of the planning process.

Getting to know public decision makers takes time and networking skills, especially because elected officials come and go, and some projects extend through several election cycles. In addition, many local government councils must abide by "sunshine" or other laws that prohibit discussions of specific projects in any venue except official hearings. Other communities frown upon wheeling and dealing with elected officials after applications for approval have been submitted. This means that developers who want to impress public officials with their intentions for developing quality projects must lay that foundation prior to or aside from discussions about specific projects. Over time, developers tend to build a network of friends who can put in a good word at the right time, if not for a specific project then at least—and significantly—about the quality of development a developer has produced in the past.

Staff of administrative agencies also care about community image but are employed to ensure that proposed projects toe the line when it comes to meeting regulatory requirements. That means that they tend to be detail-oriented and will want to know as much about projects as they can, if only to head off poorly conceived projects before they absorb too much staff time. Also, meeting with them before interviewing community leaders is a good idea because they will then have information about the project when calls begin coming in to city hall. Since planning staff usually are the professional buffer between legislators and the public, they tend to view themselves as proponents—and definers—of high-quality development. Also, the larger the staff the more specialized it becomes, so that project reviews may involve several staff members who concentrate on narrow interests.

It pays for developers to know and listen to administrative staff members. Not only is it helpful to have their support when the project comes up for approval, but also they can recommend project alterations and procedural paths that can save time and money. Chances are that they have shepherded similar projects through the approval process and know what will fly and what won't get off the ground. Often, but not always, they have the ear of the elected officials and talk to them regularly. They respect developers who do great projects and their informal indications to decision makers about developers who are dedicated to doing a good job can go a long way when it comes time for project decisions.

Generally, it is not difficult to meet and know agency staffs, most particularly on a professional level. They are interested in development and constantly interact with development firms, and are probably familiar with the reputations of planning and design consultants doing the detailed work. In their positions they may be wary of close friendship with the people they are charged with regulating, and they tend to have long memories about developers involved in poor-quality projects. But agency staffs are usually the most development-friendly people in the community. All the engagement processes profiled in the case studies attracted significant participation by professional staff of city and county agencies,

...commissioners

{are best approached when a developer has no project needing approval but may have concerns about the approval process or about commission policies concerning certain types of development.}

which saw involvement not only as a duty but as an opportunity to help shape plans.

Planning commissions provide another layer of decision making for many projects. Depending again on local laws, planning commissions often are responsible for reviewing and making recommendations on plan amendments, zoning amendments, and subdivision approvals. Frequently, commission agendas are the first public notice of projects submitted for official approval, and commission hearings are the first test of whether projects are likely to obtain approval relatively painlessly. Planning commissioners are appointed by the jurisdiction's mayor and/or council, and therefore tend to be politically connected. Generally, they are a mixed bag, representing various community interests such as neighborhood and special-interest advocates and sometimes including architects and other people directly involved in development. They may know little about the community's planning and regulatory laws and responsibilities except what they have personally encountered. If that is the case, recommendations of a planning commission may not carry much weight with elected officials. However, in some jurisdictions planning commissions are serious players in decision making about community development—meaning that elected officials seldom override commission decisions. Planning commissions are often subject to the same sunshine laws as elected officials. Thus, commissioners are best approached when a developer has no project needing approval but may have concerns about the approval process or about commission policies concerning certain types of development.

Influential Leaders

Often the people with the most influence on development decisions are already ensconced in local government, in one of the positions described above. The top planning administrator, for instance, or the city manager will usually have decided views on what makes "community-friendly" projects. Their observations about the types of development they are seeking can be quite helpful. However, throughout the community, other leaders may have considerable influence, people who have held responsible positions or who have been active in civic life and whose views are respected. Land use attorney Dwight Merriam says consulting with these people is "grass-tops" involvement; "[W]e look higher than the grass roots," he says; "we go to that stratum at the local level where we find the opinion-leaders."[1] They may be important business leaders, community activists for various causes, heads of neighborhood groups, highly regarded representatives of special-interest groups, or former longtime elected officials. Their opinions often carry a great deal of weight in strategic community decisions or they may be viewed as a neighborhood leader whose opinions others respect. Whoever they are, they generally have many years of service and have become an institutional memory for the cause or the area.

"Regular" People

Besides recognized community leaders, the residents and employees in the area surrounding the proposed project represent a constituency whose views are just as important as the "fat cats'." If energized by neighborhood activists to support or oppose a project, they can affect the balance of political power. They constitute one set of potential participants that the community engagement process would hope to attract, although they may prove reticent about taking part in large meetings. If so, their views can be sampled by door-to-door interviews or neighborhood surveys. Developers have been known to simply walk down the street and chat with folks in their yards. Arranging with a neighborhood leader for a small gathering in someone's living room can be an effective communications tool as well.

Identify Community Attitudes and Expectations

While some perceptions about development seem to be universal, different locations and scenarios will generate different concerns. What, specifically, is at issue in the case of your project? Small-group meetings can be used to take the pulse of a community, and also to describe in a more casual way some of the project's potential benefits.

How are leaders identified? By asking questions of people in the know. Developers can start by discussing the question with other developers or builders. One of the significant values that consultants add to the development team is their knowledge of who is important to talk to, who has information to share, and whose opinion can influence events. The heads of the local building industry association, the local Realtor's association, the chamber of commerce, or the downtown partnership often are good sources of information. Influential leaders can identify the movers and shakers who can help or hurt a project, key people in positions with leverage to generate support or opposition. They can be particularly helpful in pointing out the most trustworthy leaders in neighborhoods where various individuals and groups are jockeying for position.

Developers generally are skilled at networking: a conversation with one source can provide leads to other sources. Through this process, developers can identify the people who seem to have the most clout, whose knowledge and contacts are most respected, and who can play important roles in the process.

IN THE COURSE OF IDENTIFYING people with influence over development decisions, developers will be sounding them out about community attitudes and issues concerning development in general and the project in particular. The goal of these discussions with community leaders is to define concerns that may influence the approval or disapproval of the project.

Different Places, Different Issues

It should be expected that reactions to development proposals will vary from place to place, depending on the general character of the area. For example, a project proposed for a greenfields site where development is just beginning to occur, amid working farms and scattered small settlements, presents a range of interests distributed over a fairly large area. Indeed, it may be difficult to pin down just what the "community" is and whether it has any unified outlook at all. Some residents hoping to develop their own properties and others wishing to preserve their bucolic environment will raise fundamental policy issues about growth and development. Infrastructure and environmental issues are likely to be uppermost.

By contrast, a project to be located within a built-up urbanized area affects a different circle of interests. Residents living near the site will be concerned with how the project may change their neighborhood and will give close attention to micro-scale impacts. Organized neighborhood groups and business interests will carefully scrutinize the proposal. Representation of community interests may be centered in a few well-known leaders but may be fractionalized among a wide variety of people with special concerns. McCormack Baron Salazar, in Pittsburgh's Crawford Square and other similar projects across the nation, has perfected the technique of attracting members of all these types of groups to participate in planning for rehabilitation and redevelopment. Early in the planning process, the firm assembles a working advisory group to help formulate plans and to carry the torch for revitalization. As members of the community and neighborhood, participants understand they have a stake in making the project both livable and workable.

Differences will be found as well in developing suburban areas familiar with zoning wars, commercial and business centers desiring growth, and small towns undergoing rapid change that is at once exciting and worrisome. In Missoula, developer Bob Brugh knew he had to sell the concept of traditional design to local officials and neighbors of his planned development. He also needed to encourage owners of adjoining properties to allow street connections to make the project work. For his project, community engagement became a means of establishing familiarity with and assent to an unusual design approach that would unify residential and commercial components with the surrounding built-up area.

The Eastern Cambridge workshops drew neighborhood leaders and other residents into the planning process.

For community engagement programs, the point is that one outreach strategy will not fit all situations. As one reviewer of this text commented, "You don't try to do Texas-style development in California."

Developers know that some perceptions seem to be absolute: more growth will increase traffic congestion; innovative forms of development will threaten neighbors' property values; all bad effects will happen tomorrow. Other issues rise and fall as specific projects are proposed: a cherished open space will be built upon; a particular road intersection will be impacted. The Pleasant Hill experience demonstrates how, over time, perceptions change: higher-density development became more acceptable when moderated by a reduced density limit; traffic was a problem but transit-focused development offered the possibility of some relief. Similarly, the Eastern Cambridge Study Committee came into being due to citizens' fears about the amount of new development allowed by zoning in the area. They were prepared to drastically downgrade densities. However, as they understood the increase in walkability and transit-friendliness of higher-density development, they became more tolerant of intensive development as a means of stimulating non-auto travel. Pleasant Hill also shows how the development context can change: transit-oriented development is now considered a smart way to grow; market forces are stimulating Pleasant Hill's maturation as a regional activity center. The lesson of both experiences is that conditions, perceptions, attitudes, and leadership change over time. Developers know how often the preceding project paved the way for innovations in the next project.

The Art of Surfacing Issues

Developers can dig through the newspapers, surf the Web, or talk to friendly contacts to identify current issues. Have local residents fought past proposals for development on this site? Opposed similar projects? What seem to be typical red-flag concerns? What rezoning proposals got turned down in the last couple of years? This kind of information will give developers a sense of the context of the process they are about to embark on. It will also provide some background information on community attitudes toward development that will be useful in conversations with community leaders. According to Dwight Merriam, a good reconnaissance of what the public wants will turn up unsuspected issues. "I guarantee that in almost every instance you will be surprised at your own misperceptions of what is important to the community." [2]

Developer discussions with community leaders should be conceived as two-way learning opportunities. The developer needs to be alerted to hot-button development issues that are on many minds, while the leader being interviewed wants to hear how the project can benefit the community. Usually the best situations in which to surface these topics are individual or small-group discussions in an informal setting. Every developer will have his or her own way to introduce the subject

Potential residents insisted on a variety of distinctive home designs that would contribute to the neighborliness of the Crawford Square redevelopment.

but, hopefully, topics of conversation will include:

- Where the community leader fits into the decision making process—what positions he or she has held, what interests in community development;
- A briefing about the principal features of the project, conveying the community benefits that will be achieved and the preparations for a community engagement process;
- A plain-spoken discussion about concerns that have been raised about the project, the leader's assessment of them, and how they can be avoided or allayed;
- General community development issues that can affect the acceptance of the project, such as concerns about rapid growth, loss of open space, or lack of funds for needed schools or sewers;
- Any hints about project features that community leaders really admire or really detest;
- News about upcoming changes in policies or regulations.

It is important that the developer avoid coming across as a high-powered salesperson, pushing all the virtues of the project while soft-pedaling its potential effects. Sounding like a "typical" developer raises warning flags for most people. Listening is vital for developers. In this situation, it is usually more effective to receive as well as give information. Community leaders can describe the prevailing sentiments among community leadership about growth and development—which types or aspects of development will stir instant opposition and which will be greeted with enthusiasm. They can give examples of specific issues that arose in recently proposed projects and how they were resolved. They can suggest aspects of the proposed project that will be attractive to particular leaders. If prompted ("What about this project do you especially like?"), they might suggest how to describe the project in compelling terms that will attract support.

This kind of information can also be obtained or augmented through an opinion survey or poll. Many public affairs and marketing firms have experience in making surveys and, if questions are properly framed, the results can be extremely helpful as a sample of a fairly large group of affected stakeholders. Of course, questions can be artfully skewed to obtain the "right" answers, but a survey or poll by a reputable firm can deliver solid information about local views on current issues. In Park City, the polling consultant found that a majority of residents were inclined to support rather than oppose the proposed ski resort project, and were more likely to support it if certain aspects of the project (such as protected open space) were expanded. That information provided a key to the developer's actions in seeking project approval.

It is important that the developer avoid coming across as a high-powered salesperson, pushing all the virtues of the project while soft-pedaling its potential effects.

Checkpoint

Now it's time to tally up the results of your research and determine the project's viability in the community. If it looks doable, you're ready to embark on an outreach process.

WITH THE INFORMATION ASSEMBLED during this initial phase of community engagement, developers can pause to add up the pluses and minuses of launching a project on this site. Are the pluses strong enough to carry the day when measured against the minuses? Can negative impacts be offset by adding design features or altering the makeup of uses? Would the neighborhood or community value the contribution of a community amenity that might also improve the marketability of the project? Are these modifications financially feasible?

If the answers to the questions in the preceding paragraph are negative, the developer has some serious thinking to do about the nature of the project and the likelihood of obtaining public approval to move ahead. If the answers are mostly or entirely positive, the developer has in hand, with the definition of an overall strategy, the basic information needed to begin organizing a public outreach process.

CHECKLIST

✓ To set up the framework for the process, answer the following three questions: What outcome am I hoping to achieve? What issues might arise from site conditions and the project's possible impacts? Who are the people who should participate in the process?

✓ Learn about the community firsthand by researching its history, walking it, observing, and talking with locals. Casual, small-group meetings, like a coffee hour held in a local resident's home, can be helpful for getting and giving information.

✓ Compile solid data, perhaps with the help of consultants, to supplement the information thus gathered.

✓ Determine the project's viability in the community based on findings.

Part III Making It Happen: Achieving Community Acceptance

Setting Up the Engagement Process

Line up a publicity program early to get the word out about the process and keep people informed of its ongoing progress. Be ready to disseminate basic information culled from studies that address likely concerns and project benefits. Helpful studies can be those outlining real estate market, traffic, environmental, economic, and historic issues.

AT THIS POINT IN THE PROCESS, the developer will possess a fairly complete concept of the project, including its components, size, and design parameters. The developer will also know who the key participants in the outreach process are likely to be and the issues they will bring to the table. Now it's time to begin setting up the community engagement process.

The centerpiece, of course, will be the series of meetings that directly engage participants. A dynamic communications program should be worked out early to publicize the engagement process, its findings, and conclusions.

To first engage the community, generate technical data about the project area and its potential effects on the community—positive *and* negative. In all of the case studies, consultants and participants found it helpful to have basic studies supporting the realities of identified issues and the opportunities offered by site and area conditions. Indeed, most engagement processes begin with a factual presentation of existing conditions in the site or area, but detailed questions may well emerge during discussions. In the Eastern Cambridge research, for example, the consultants prepared, prior to the series of workshops, detailed information about traffic congestion and vacant sites—two issues they knew would come up right away. As a result, they were able to nip threatening concerns in the bud, namely by showing that most traffic that was congesting major streets represented through trips rather than neighborhood-generated trips. Additional development, in other words, would not be likely to drastically increase congestion. The consultants were also able to demonstrate that a considerable amount of vacant or underused land outside existing neighborhoods was available to permit substantial new development. This information was key to alleviating residents' fears about the impacts of further development in the area.

Which specific studies should be undertaken depends on the critical issues identified during the strategy-setting phase of the process. Real estate market studies are often important to assure citizens engaged in discussions that certain types of development are necessary and marketable. Traffic studies that show street volumes and congestion spots are commonly of interest. Other information about environmental concerns, fiscal issues, or historic design features may be appropriate. Much of this information may be available from public or published sources, but some may require on-site evaluations and even input from residents.

Summation of Critical Traffic Movements (Trips) Above Desired Threshold

Scenarios	Critical Movements Above Threshold
Status Quo (existing zoning)	2,530
Citywide Rezoning	1,650
Initial Land Use Plan	1,290
Preferred Trip Reduction Scenario	920

The Eastern Cambridge consultants answered concerns about traffic by showing residents that the proposed development would produce fewer additional vehicle trips than existing zoning, as well as previous planning and zoning proposals.

GROUND RULES FOR A COLLABORATIVE PROCESS

Collaborative outreach processes tackle complex but negotiable issues involving a number of parties who are willing to work with rather than against one another. The aim is to build a common understanding of the existing and forecast circumstances of the area under consideration, develop and test ideas, and design workable and reasonable solutions that will gain general support. That goal is accomplished through following some rules that may appear simple but can be difficult to apply:

- Participation is inclusive, with representation from all parties with a stake in the results;
- Participants are responsible for ensuring the success of the process;
- Discussion proceeds only after agreement on a common sense of the purpose and problem is reached;
- Participants help to educate each other about issues, concerns, and opportunities—all ideas are heard;
- Options are not optional: many options are identified and evaluated;
- Decisions are made by general agreement, not by voting that creates winners and losers; disagreements should be noted;
- Participants understand that they will share in implementing the solutions;
- Participants and the public are kept informed about the process and its results.[1]

Identifying an Official Convener

With a fund of basic information established, organizing the outreach process requires four tasks:

(1) Determining the appropriate convener of the process;
(2) Identifying the types and sequence of events that will enable participants to air their concerns and interests and, by engaging in public discussions, will lead to agreement on project goals and a plan;
(3) Establishing the appropriate roles of the participants, based on knowledge of their interests determined during the initial phase of the process; and
(4) Assembling the consultant team necessary to accomplish the goals of the process.

Because these tasks are closely interrelated, process organizers probably will outline several scenarios defining variations on the "who, what, and when" of the process before reaching a conclusion. Even then, it is a given that during the process itself, needs for changes and additions will arise. Process organizers know ahead of time that the process must be flexible and responsive to the learning that takes place.

Participants will look on the convener as the party who cares the most about what happens to the project. No matter who takes the lead—developers, public or nonprofit agencies, task forces, or consultants—developers should stay in constant contact with key decision makers in the community.

DEVELOPERS PUTTING TOGETHER a community engagement process should give some thought to selecting the person or organization to be publicly identified as the sponsor or convener of the process. Normally, the convener will take a lead role in managing the process and be visibly involved throughout; most important, participants will view the convener as the person or entity with the greatest concern about the quality of the results. Conveners can be a public agency or nonprofit group with a clear stake in the results, or a task force appointed to make recommendations on the issue, or a highly reputable community leader known for interest in community development.

In many circumstances, state or local statutes will prevent public officials and staff from assuming a leadership role in the engagement process, particularly if they will later be making official decisions concerning its approval. In some communities they will be dissuaded from even attending the public meetings, although they may be briefed in separate work sessions. Public staff members, however, are usually able to attend events to act as technical resources.

In the case of developer-driven processes, the most obvious choice for the convener is the developer. After all, the developer frequently will want to be personally involved in winning friends and influencing the recommendations issuing from the process. There are advantages to putting the developer up front where he or she can be accessible, engaged, and clearly concerned with obtaining community input to a proposed project. The developer's personality is a key determinant. Developers who come across as sincere, thoughtful, and willing to entertain new ideas can sway opinions and elicit positive responses to issues. They add credibility to the process and the results. Alternatively, developers who appear the least bit arrogant, opinionated, and set in their ways can generate negative feelings about the project. The developer's staff or consultants can suggest that the latter take a background role in the proceedings, speaking out from time to time with positive and carefully phrased observations rather than stern lectures about the difficulties of the development business.

Developers need the participation or interest of local public officials in the process. If the proposed project is likely to involve provision of public improvements, construction of public buildings, or special approval processes, representatives of those departments can be brought into a formal or informal working group that functions as a coordinator of key decisions about the project. Or if the local government has formed a task force to pursue answers to a development question, the task force can be named as the sponsor or convener of an outreach process. The Pleasant Hill process technically was sponsored by the two public entities and the developer with the principal control over prospective development, but the appointed task force acted as the publicly visible group in reaching agreement on recommendations. As in Pleasant Hill, such a process is often set up to keep the "background sponsors" aware of progress on project plans and designs and upcoming needs for official reviews, which can smooth the path to public approvals. In addition, consultants managing the charrette processes conducted in several of the case study projects regularly checked ideas about proposed public facility improvements with city officials.

Most often, developers choose to take a step back from active participation and form a consultant team to take the lead (and the heat) in convening and managing the process. In addition to obtaining the services of the typical range of design, marketing, and other specialists, they can engage consultants with recognized skills in organizing outreach programs. The consultant team can then be positioned as the developer's representative in charge of managing the process. Developers can still take part in the process but act more as observers and commentators rather than as managers directly involved in decision making. But they will become a familiar and friendly presence and can be primed to step forward as final decisions are being made to signal a strong interest in positive results.

In any of these circumstances, whether developers, public or nonprofit agencies, task forces, or a consultant team take the lead in managing the process, developers should maintain frequent contact with key decision makers in the community. This can be implemented through individual conversations with key leaders by developers or their consultants, or the creation of an unofficial working group of local leaders to explore major issues, identify their priorities, check major decisions, and try out ideas.

Determining Appropriate Types of Events

- **Public meetings and forums bring large or small groups together for discussion, brainstorming, and even taking straw votes.**
- **Charrettes and workshops involve recurring evaluations of evolving plans and designs, with the object being agreement on a final concept.**
- **Targeted discussions allow close examination of a particular issue.**
- **Focus groups assess public opinions.**
- **Tours can be used to gather information and communicate development and design concepts.**

CITIZEN ENGAGEMENT EVENTS consist of one or more types of settings that will encourage participants to enter into discussions, draw out their views and concerns, consider project proposals, generate useful responses and, ultimately, support a proposed project. Typical settings include:

- Meetings and forums, large and small, suitable for conveying information, obtaining feedback, and generating ideas from participants;
- Charrettes and other types of hands-on workshops to engage participants in determining project plans and designs;
- Focus groups and other targeted discussions to obtain ideas and advice on specific topics or issues;
- Tours of the area or other areas that can serve as examples.

Public Meetings and Forums

Known by many different names, these types of events foster communication between event organizers and a generally self-selected group of participants. Their main function is to provide opportunities for interactive discussion among the various participants, bringing large or small groups together to learn about project proposals, voice concerns and issues, offer ideas and support, and even take straw votes on the popularity of project proposals or details. A common technique today is staging plenary sessions of the whole group with smaller break-out discussions to focus on specific concerns and report findings back to the plenary session.

Large public meetings are useful for conveying basic information about projects—among other purposes to dispel rumors—and for hearing about concerns and interests. But as a discussion format they are difficult to guide and may detour into complaint sessions that fix negative images in participants' minds. Small-group meetings enhance opportunities for participants to engage in free-ranging, interactive discussions. They frequently generate fresh ideas or perspectives on project concepts that lead to improved plans. Members of small groups can be chosen by self selection according to participant interests, by random assignments of participants, or by conscious selection of participants to provide a range of interests in each group. Consultants for the Eastern Cambridge charrette preselected groups for the discussion tables to ensure the trading of information and views among a variety of interests.

Meetings of any size must have a recognizable product that can be summarized at the end to provide a stepping-stone toward the next meeting.

Occasionally, pulling together small groups to focus on special issues can resolve potential conflicts before they become obstacles to agreements.

Charrettes and Workshops

Architecture students applied the French term "charrette" to the intensive all-night efforts necessary to complete assignments on deadline. Now the term is used as well to refer to concentrated efforts involving a group of self-selected participants to study and complete a plan or design for a development project within a short time frame. (Some consultants prefer to call them design workshops.) Typically spread over several days or a week, charrettes and workshops engage participants in recurring evaluations of evolving plans and designs, with the object to agree on a final concept by the end of the period. The consultant team establishes a conveniently located design studio for the duration, allowing them to interact with participants during meetings or as local residents find time to drop in to review the latest design iterations.

As the case studies demonstrate, the typical sequence of events will be organized to initially convey basic information about the project—location, general character, size, elements, design, relationships to surrounding areas, etc.—then move into eliciting participants' responses to attributes they find attractive, others they would like to see improved or altered, and still others they object to. The developer and consultant team will respond to these points with revised designs, and continuing discussions hopefully will generate fairly common agreement on a reasonable proposal. Small-group or focus-group discussions may be utilized to allow more intensive examination of important concerns.

The National Charrette Institute, based in Portland, Oregon, advocates at least three design cycles leading from initial sketches of alternative design approaches, to revisions (or major changes), to a final plan. Each cycle (the institute's Bill Lennertz calls them "feedback loops") includes an evaluation period by charrette participants, ranging from responses to public presentations to one-on-one discussions with designers at "pin-up" sessions, where the latest sketches are pinned on the walls before small-group sessions discussing difficult issues. The process puts a premium on visible collaboration between the consultant team and local participants, through the on-site availability and work of the design team. It also emphasizes a multidisciplinary, holistic approach to producing a feasible plan. After a final plan is presented at the end of the charrette, the plan is tested further with local experts on technical questions. Within a few weeks, the consultants return for a final public presentation, which effectively launches the action phase of project development.[2]

Charrettes are particularly useful for areas and projects in which community leaders are prepared to back well-designed development. The North St. Lucie County charrette, for example, used a variety of visualization techniques to illustrate the clustering of future development as an alternative to continuing sprawl. Charrette participants, having agreed with basic principles for conserving open space and clustering development, were ready to support the resulting plan. Participants in the Missoula charrette, excited by the opportunity to take part in planning an innovative mixed-use development, joined in discussions that led to an approved design. The Nashville charrette got off to a strong start because many participants had previously taken part in such events; they understood the rules of the game and were enthusiastic about offering suggestions.

Charrettes are particularly useful for areas and projects in which community leaders are prepared to back well-designed development.

Charrettes have become popular in part due to the increasing emphasis in planning circles on the value of urban design—of basing development decisions on detailed site and building designs that reflect superior architectural and planning practices. The growth in popular respect for new

The Pleasant Hill charrette provided participants with plenty of opportunities to probe details of alternative design.

urbanist and neotraditional concepts of building and site design has tended to diffuse the supposed threats of "urban" development, such as density and a mix of uses.

The charrette process builds on participatory planning processes used since the 1970s to resolve development disputes and reach agreements on plans and action programs by forming collaborative relationships between planners and neighborhood residents. One difference is the day-to-day, even hour-to-hour working relationship established between design technicians and at least some charrette participants; another difference is the compressed time frame, which introduces pressures for reaching agreement quickly. However, charrettes are not a cure-all for overcoming entrenched opposition, or where the wisdom of development of any kind is being debated, says Debra Stein, a development marketing expert. She contends that charrettes are likely to attract participants who want to protect their existing quality of life by resisting projects that will bring major change to the neighborhood.[3] Still, because charrettes involve local interests in plan-making for development, they can help to win support for the plans and designs they produce.

CHARRETTE STRATEGIES

(Based on "What is a Charrette?" at www.lcaarchitects.com, LCA Town Planning and Architecture, LLC, now part of HDR/LCA and Sargent Town Planning)

1. Work collaboratively: Create a long-lived plan based on each individual's unique contributions.

2. Design cross-functionally: Multidisciplinary teams work concurrently to build a feasible solution from the beginning.

3. Use design to achieve a shared vision and create holistic solutions: Design illustrates the complexity of the problem and can be used to resolve conflict by proposing previously unexplored solutions that represent win/win outcomes.

4. Study the details and the whole: Lasting agreement is based on a fully informed dialogue.

5. Compress work schedules: Time compression facilitates creative problem solving by accelerating decision making and reducing unconstructive negotiation tactics.

6. Communicate in short feedback loops: Regular stakeholder reviews quickly build trust in the process and foster true understanding and support of the product.

7. Work over at least four to seven consecutive days: Four days are required to accommodate three feedback loops, which are the minimum required to facilitate a change in participants' perceptions and positions.

8. Hold the charrette on site: Working on site fosters participants' understanding of local values and traditions and provides the necessary access to stakeholders and information.

9. Produce a buildable plan: The success of a community's work to plan and build together hinges on implementation tools such as codes and regulating plans as well as recognizing market and financial realities.

10. Evaluate the plan with objective measures: Determine appropriate measures to qualify and quantify the plans, from concept development through the final plan.[4]

"Pin-up" sessions organized during the North St. Lucie County charrette put maps and drawings up so that citizens could browse through the latest ideas from the consultant team, with team members available to respond to questions and comments.

Targeted Discussions

Discussions conducted in typical meetings and charrettes roam widely across all aspects of development proposals. By contrast, small-group meetings are organized to delve into targeted issue areas. Targeted group meetings allow close examination of a particular issue associated with a proposed development—for example, one that involves assessments of technical information or evaluations of findings from detailed studies. Several of the case study charrettes scheduled special meetings to consider traffic issues. These events brought technical experts, including city staff that would implement the results, together with the participants most interested in the topic to work out feasible solutions. In the North St. Lucie charrette, the consultants discovered that county planning staff had views about the use of transferable development rights as incentives for rural clustering that diverged from the intentions of the design team and charrette participants. The consultants pulled together county officials and staff to meet with selected participants to air differences and reach agreement on a strategy. The meeting helped avoid a political confrontation over the issue.

Such small-group meetings frequently are organized quickly during the outreach process to respond to issues as they arise, but they can be scheduled as part of a process when it is clear that one or more prominent concerns will need special attention. Generally, small-group meetings are relatively brief, from one or two hours up to a half day, but can be organized as a short series of meetings. They tend to be most successful when focused on answering a specific question: To what degree will traffic congestion increase? What visual impacts on the surrounding neighborhoods will the proposed buildings have? How can various parks and open spaces be connected to form a greenway?

The participants ordinarily are selected for their technical knowledge or representation of key interests concerned with the issue to be discussed. Groups can include a few participants up to 20 or 25—no more numerous than can be expected to sustain a spirited, interactive discussion among all attendees. Meetings may be informal but still should be guided by a capable leader and an agenda that promises to yield a satisfactory result.

Focus Groups

Focus groups have been used extensively by marketing firms, including those working for builders, to test consumer reaction to new products and services. The concept is being found increasingly useful in assessing public opinions on aspects of proposed development projects. Group participants are chosen to represent the variety of stakeholders affected by the development. A facilitator asks questions—"What home designs do you especially like?" "Do you like the idea of keeping parking behind stores?"—and gauges the interests and reactions of the participants. Conversation between participants is encouraged. Focus groups often can be very satisfying for participants; after all, who doesn't like being asked his opinion? The buy-in of participants to the results can expand support for the final product of the community engagement process.

Generally, small-group meetings are relatively brief, from one or two hours up to a half day, but can be organized as a short series of meetings. They tend to be most successful when focused on answering a specific question.

Tours

Tours are useful in a number of ways. They can be undertaken as research and information-gathering efforts, or as methods of communicating development and design concepts and best practices. But most turn into events in which participants learn about the project area or exemplary similar projects, then use the occasion to discuss the comparable qualities of what they are seeing and what they know about the proposed project. Developers can use tours of the project area to point out how proposed projects will relate to the surrounding area and to give participants more than a virtual experience of site features. They can tour attractive, on-the-ground examples of design concepts similar to those proposed in the project. With a little luck and perhaps some preplanning, tour groups can hear from local residents about how well the development will fit into the neighborhood. Alternatively, "virtual tours" of top-notch projects can be presented by developers brought in from other cities.

The Park City Mining Company offered tours of the mine on the site as something of a door prize for receiving information about the project and being shown around the site. The mine had little to do with the proposed project, but was a historic curiosity that participants enjoyed visiting while learning about the proposed development. Tours have a way of bringing proposals alive for people who otherwise may have trouble visualizing the completed development.

Managing Events

Presentations will address participant interests and concerns, and meeting facilitation by informed and capable leaders or trained, knowledgeable professionals can accomplish this constructively. Competent management with a personable touch will help coax participants to become involved, share ideas and views, and reach agreement.

ALL OF THESE EVENT formats will benefit from skilled introductions, presentations, and discussion facilitation. Whoever is assigned the opening statement must establish the purpose, character, and guiding rules of behavior for the meeting in a welcoming, hopeful manner. This is the time to seize participants' interest and lay out an agenda that promises to utilize their knowledge and talents. The opener establishes the desired end product of the event as a goal worthy of everyone's involvement.

It goes without saying that presentations must be mindful of the desired conclusion of the process: a feasible, marketable, and desirable project. But presentations must avoid suggesting that aspects of proposals are not negotiable until they have been subjected

Preliminary sketches such as this one of the northern area in Eastern Cambridge help to illustrate ideas under discussion during a charrette.

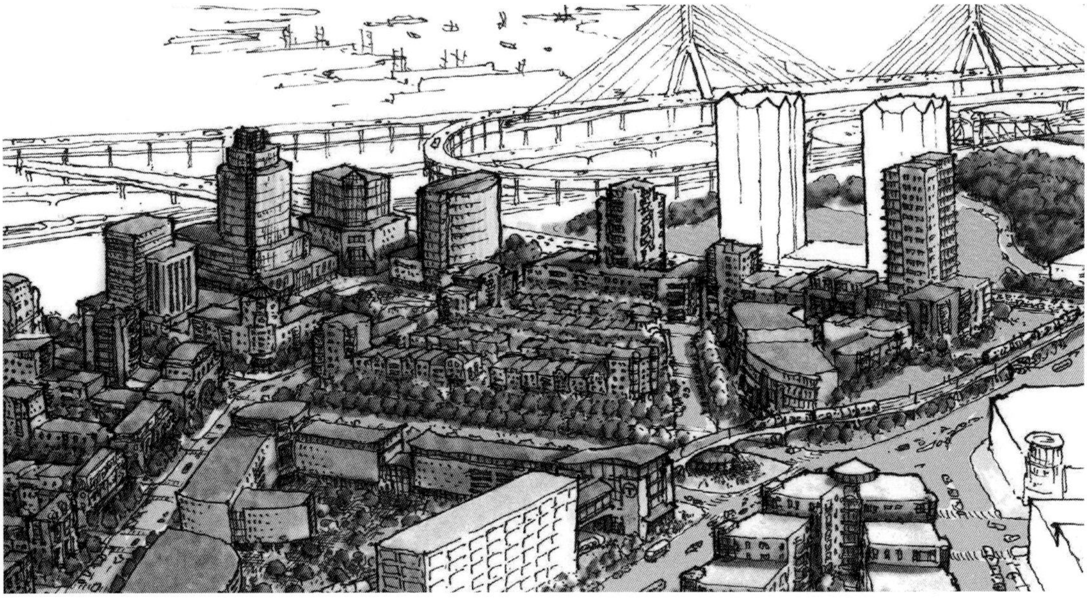

THE BASICS OF MEETING ORGANIZATION AND CONDUCT

Location and Setting: Formal rooms (such as the council hearing room in city hall) will tend to dampen free discussion. Instead, find a conference room or other space that conveys a neutral spirit in which people can feel at ease. Arrange chairs, tables, lighting, and other equipment to enhance group interaction. Meetings to convey information can be set up classroom style, but meetings intended to promote interactive discussions should enable participants to look at each other while talking.

Equipment: Certainty is a blessing in the hustle and bustle of meetings, so keeping it simple is often the best strategy. If elaborate arrays of equipment are necessary for the task at hand, keep in mind that they will require extra care to set up and knowledgeable staff to quickly fix any problems that might occur. Test all equipment beforehand and be sure to come armed with fallback resources (e.g., handouts).

Tone: Speakers should speak slowly and clearly, using plain language and adding a humorous point now and then. Communication only occurs when the audience truly understands the speaker, so lose the jargon and make sure to explain anything that might appear elusive or overly technical. Know what's likely to turn your audience on or off: go with a glossy presentation, or perhaps something more down-home?

Timing: Pick a starting time that will be convenient for most of the expected participants—whether first thing in the morning, on their way home from work, or after an early dinner. Announce and honor the ending time so participants will stay for the whole meeting. Relieve anxieties by noting that staff will be available after the meeting to answer specific questions.

Expectations: Tell participants the major subject of the meeting and brief them on what events have occurred previously to get to the point. Let them know how they are expected to participate—as listeners, questioners, discussants, and/or planner/designers; in plenary and/or small-group discussions. Tell them how the results of the meeting will be recorded or summarized and reported to others.

Ground Rules: Participants should remember to speak one at a time, to allow disagreement without rancor, to cite examples, to point out needs for information, and to allow others to speak.

Introduce Participants: If a large group, describe the range of interests of participants known to be attending, or ask for a show of hands to indicate their backgrounds or interests. If a small group, have them introduce themselves in a few words. Avoid creating opportunities for grandstanding or speeches.

Assign and Identify Support Staff: Anticipate needs for equipment operators, small-group facilitators and reporters, notetakers, greeters, handout helpers, etc. Determine whether you'll need technical staff to assist at this stage. Introduce staff when appropriate during the meeting so they can be recognized at subsequent meetings.

to open discussion. It is best to approach project proposals as preliminary ideas awaiting comment, adjustment, and improvement. Most important, presentations must address, directly or discretely, the interests and concerns of the participants.

Meeting facilitation by informed and capable leaders is also important. Ideally, facilitators are trained, personable, stimulating, and knowledgeable about the content of the discussions. These qualities will help them coax participants to become involved, share ideas and views, and reach agreement. Small-group discussions may be facilitated by respected community leaders known to be familiar with the subject and willing to solicit ideas rather than preach solutions.

AVOIDING HOSTILE MEETINGS

Debra Stein, GCA Strategies, Inc.

It's every developer's nightmare: an audience of furious neighbors booing, throwing wads of paper, and shouting "Not in my back yard!" Fortunately, there are a variety of tools that developers can use to avoid negative emotions and angry behavior.

Don't Make 'Em Mad

Anger is a symptom of an underlying, negative emotion: people are really mad about something else. In an audience setting, the negative circumstances most likely to trigger citizen fury are frustration, humiliation, and unpleasant environmental conditions.

Frustration: When people think they have been unfairly treated they get frustrated and then they get mad. Real estate development is intrinsically frustrating for neighbors because people living near the project site frequently experience a disproportionate level of negative impacts without enjoying disproportionate benefits, and that seems unfair. Large community meetings can also produce frustration and anger. Most neighbors show up expecting to speak, but often get stuck listening to the developer and waiting for their turn instead. Developers can minimize disappointment and resulting anger by making certain that participants have realistic expectations about how the meeting will run: "I have a 20-minute presentation that describes the project and then I'd like to hear what you think about it." Answer questions realistically, identifying sources of information if possible, and admit that some questions have no answers at the present time. Also explain actions that may seem arbitrary or unfair, such as letting some people who must leave early speak before others.

Loss of Face: People get angry when they feel insulted, manipulated, talked down to, or made to look ridiculous. Choose language carefully to avoid overly technical lingo that most people will not understand. In a university study of anger, 64 percent of angry people reported that they behave aggressively in order to repair their damaged self-image or enhance their self-esteem. Interestingly, women are more likely than men to get angry when they feel condescended to or ignored. Respectful treatment of audiences is always important, especially in volatile situations.

Environmental Conditions: Research confirms that people are much more likely to feel angry when exposed to unpredictable noise, strange music, high temperatures, or bad smells such as cigarette smoke. Intense crowding or inability to hear the speaker or see the slide screen can also lead to stress and resulting anger. When a meeting is likely to stir controversy, it's important to pick the best environment possible.

Negative Signals: You can tell that the audience is experiencing negative emotions when participants display a very reliable signal of their feelings—covering their mouths with their hands while listening. When you see this, change your communications approach or shift subjects immediately.

Avoid Nasty Behavior

Just because someone feels angry doesn't necessarily mean that person has to behave in an angry manner. There are several practical steps you can take to avoid hostile conduct, even when emotions are running high.

Set Ground Rules: Before launching into a presentation, take a few moments to set ground rules about how this portion of the meeting is going to run—meeting rules typically include prohibitions on shouting, interruptions, profanity, or personal insults—and detail the procedure and timing for audience questions or comments. It is crucial, however, to get the audience to "buy into" your rules: "Is there anyone here who doesn't understand these rules and agree to follow them?" Obtaining consensus on the ground rules makes it much easier to enforce them if people start behaving badly.

Maintain Eye Contact: It is easier to lash out at an impersonal, faceless enemy than to attack someone with whom one has a personal relationship. You can significantly decrease the chances that an audience will treat you badly if you can force participants to engage in eye contact with you, increasing the chance that people will engage in personal interaction with you.

Eliminate Anonymity: People are more likely to engage in antisocial conduct when they think they're anonymous members of the crowd. Minimize aggressive behavior by making it easier to hold them personally responsible for antisocial actions. Use name tags; put out a sign-up sheet that asks for E-mail addresses; call on citizens by name. Have speakers identify themselves before each comment or question. Bright lights, mirrors, cameras, and rhetorical questions also help to reduce anonymity.

Anger Management Plan

Look before you leap. Prepare an anger management plan to anticipate possible audience problems, to develop a strategy to avoid or respond to those problems, and to rehearse your responses. Ask yourself:

- What fundamental ground rules should I suggest to maintain a civil discussion? What procedures should be used to manage audience input?
- What issues are likely to lead to a sense of frustration? How can I shape citizens' expectations so they don't get disappointed at the meeting?
- Are there any particular community leaders or activists who need lots of special attention? How will I demonstrate my respect for them?
- What can I do to make the setting as pleasant as possible?
- How can I encourage citizens to see themselves as individuals rather than anonymous members of a crowd?
- What short, effective responses can I make to the most likely types of attacks I might face at the meeting?

By anticipating audience anger and preparing an anger management plan ahead of time, developers can make sure that nightmares about furious neighbors don't turn into reality.

Structuring the Sequence of Events

The sequence of events should combine numerous small or individual meetings with key community leaders. One or two large public meetings can be held to draw the attention of the general public. Subsequent events should provide a mix of activities to continue to attract participation from a variety of interested individuals and organizations.

PROCESS ORGANIZERS NEED TO CAREFULLY organize the types, locations, and sequence of events that will lead to a general consensus on a project plan. Typically, the order and location of events will familiarize the community with the character of the proposed project, provide sound information about issues that will arise, ensure plenty of time for interactive discussions about the project and consideration of potential solutions for issues, and work toward some type of closure on the merits of the proposal. Some issues may demand special attention in small-group discussions. The number of events and their sequence will depend upon the particular circumstances of the project and the community, such as:

- *Size and complexity of the project:* A large-scale, mixed-use community development is likely to require more outreach time and intensive discussion than a small, single-use subdivision;
- *Number and importance of issues needing resolution:* Resolving several major issues probably will take time and numerous meetings, but may set up tradeoffs that can help mold decisions;
- *Extent to which community leadership is organized and experienced in outreach activities:* Experienced community leaders willing to reach agreement may favor an expedited process (unless participants enjoy the experience so much that they prolong it!); organized leadership intent on obstructing agreement may lengthen the process;
- *Number, size, and strength of community groups to be included:* If numerous competitive, powerful groups are involved, they can prolong a process indefinitely;
- *Expectations of public officials and the community at large, based on previous engagement processes for similar projects:* A procedural model already established will favor engaging in a similar process unless people are looking for a change;
- *Degree of closure required in achieving public agreement:* Obtaining general acquiescence to a proposed project may require less effort than seeking a formal approval from an official group;

- *Deadline or timeline determined by a scheduled decision point, such as adoption of a community's new comprehensive plan or zoning ordinance, or the end date of a property option or financial deal:* Such decision points often represent artificial rather than real deadlines (e.g., property options can be renewed);
- *Budget established by the developer for obtaining project approval:* It is seldom large enough but can be enlarged as support for the project becomes more tangible.

In general, the selected events and their sequence will be organized to attract participation of desirable community leaders and organizations and to work toward participants' acquiescence with a specific project proposal. Process organizers should identify the results from the various events to mark significant agreements as well as progress.

Defining Roles of Participants

Participant roles will be based on the range of community interests, who should be involved, and what needs to be resolved. Open processes allow anyone who walks through the door to participate. Formal task forces or committees place greater responsibility (and authority) on participants, while advisory or working groups are also substantive, yet less formal. Certain participants can be chosen to lead as moderators at public meetings, or facilitators at small-group functions.

PARTICIPANTS CAN PLAY A VARIETY of roles in community engagement processes. A few can be selected to act as event leaders or moderators. Some or all participants can be appointed to task forces and committees that confer special status upon them. Participants who take part as representatives of key organizations can be recognized in assignments as leaders or committee members. And individuals interested in specific issues can choose to join in small-group discussions. Organizers of community involvement processes should consider how best to engage potential participants in the process.

Planning agencies, in the pursuit of participatory democracy, may be required or may choose to let anyone who walks in the door take part in meetings. Open processes that allow anyone to participate at any time can attract a broad cross section of participants, including people who have not previously been heard from. Open meetings are useful for conveying basic information or presenting alternative plans and preliminary design ideas for review. However, they may suffer from interruptions by participants with their own agendas and difficulties with engaging participants in truly interactive discussions. To the extent that participants divert discussion from the main subject, they can drive away potential contributors of ideas and concerns. In addition, if participants come to one meeting and not others they may not be helpful in determining the outcome. These are reasons that some outreach organizers limit the number of large public events. Organizers hold some "everyone come" sessions to initiate the process, attract participants, convey information, and review final plans, but plan to work with selected smaller groups to grapple with issues and iron out design details.

A popular technique that public agencies often use to obtain citizen participation is establishing a task force and/or a set of committees to engage in discussions and make more or less formal reports to an officially recognized body. Developer-driven processes can also set up task forces and committees to represent a wide variety of interests. Public/private projects are frequently undertaken under the management of a task force or committee structure, which essentially functions as an advisory mechanism to assist decision making by public officials. Establishing such a structure confers a modicum of official status on the participants and their recommendations. The possibility of naming task force and committee chairpersons adds more opportunities for conferring status. The task force/committee-led process also suggests that participation will lead to an implementable product valued by community leaders. For this reason, members should be chosen to establish an active chemistry that will lead to valuable recommendations. Avoid padding the group to make it appear impressive.

Developers, however, may find that establishing a task force or advisory committee to engage citizens for their projects brings problems as well as opportunities. One concern is the complication of managing intergroup communications between task groups, committees, and subcommittees. That ongoing task can demand considerable investment in time and effort and lengthen the decision making process. The second problem for a developer is the relinquishment of control over project decisions to a group or groups that lack the developer's direct stake in the project. Developers who are responsible for returning a profit to investors must set ground rules that emphasize the advisory, not controlling, nature of the task. Nevertheless, in some situations the use of a well-managed task force with a lean committee structure can deliver a positive influence on final project approval.

In his book, *The Complete Guide to Zoning*, Dwight Merriam describes such a group formed by the developer of a residential life-care project targeted to empty-nesters and seniors. The proposed project was next to an established single-family home neighborhood, which ordinarily might be counted upon to object to higher-density forms of residential development. The advisory committee had no official standing but consisted of highly regarded community leaders. Their critique of early concepts for project design was helpful in shaping the project and in engaging their support for the final proposal in the public hearing. Due to their involvement as well as other outreach to the surrounding neighborhood, the project won approval even after its density was doubled to include midrise buildings.[5]

An alternative to forming a formal task force or committee structure is establishing regular interaction with what might be called a "shadow" advisory group or a working group that represents the final decision making entity. The Pleasant Hill charrette process, for example, was guided by representatives of the three client groups—the local government, the transit agency, and the designated developer. The consultants managing the community engagement process regularly acted as intermediaries between this client group and the participants in the discussion process, reporting to the client group on emerging issues and seeking guidance on their resolution. The group provided a clearinghouse for determining elements of the evolving plan.

Even open processes, however, can benefit from selection of certain participants as process leaders—for example, as moderators for public meetings or as facilitators and reporters of small-group discussions. Giving constructive community leaders some visibility in the process can indicate the developer's concern for involving the community and can help to build comradery among participants. It goes without saying that involvement of leaders also helps to win understanding and cooperation from those leaders—and their friends in high places.

In practice, most community engagement processes mix and match open and selective events to attract wide participation but bring together smaller groups to focus on resolving certain issues. The outreach strategy should determine the appropriateness of formal or informal participant roles based on the range of community interests, who should be involved, and the types of issues that demand resolution.

MOBILIZING SUPPORTERS FOR A PUBLIC HEARING

Debra Stein, GCA Strategies, Inc.

How do you get citizens to actually attend a hearing, stand up at the microphone, and tell politicians, "I support this development proposal and want you to approve it right now"? Mobilizing supporters involves six distinct steps:

1. Target Supporters: Developers often spend too much time trying to convert die-hard opponents into flag-waving supporters. When hearing time rolls around there may be plenty of people eager to testify against the project but few people willing to say, "I support this proposal!" At some point, the practical project sponsor must look beyond citizen resistance and focus on motivating and mobilizing people who will benefit from new development.

2. Create Favorable Attitudes: Developers can use a variety of persuasive techniques to create favorable attitudes about their proposals. Rational persuasion presumes that listeners have the time, interest, and ability to evaluate the facts and logical arguments about why a land use plan is good for the community. Project opponents often use *emotional* persuasion such as appeals to fear ("Our kids will get killed crossing the street"), threats ("We'll sue!"), and appeals to pity ("How could you do this to us?"). Peripheral persuasion recognizes that the external context of your communication may be more important than its internal content. For example, neighbors engaged in peripheral evaluation might simply decide that, since it seems that "everyone" hates a proposed shopping center, it must be a bad idea. Sophisticated advocacy campaigns utilize rational, emotional, and peripheral messages to shift attitudes and create pro-project beliefs—for example by showing how many school children in the new development will be able to walk to their local school on streets designed for pedestrians, or by demonstrating the variety of day-to-day service needs that will be incorporated in or near the proposed project.

3. Get an Initial Commitment: It is tempting to immediately ask a potential supporter to testify in favor of your project, but citizens are much more likely to agree to a big request for support if you can get them to first comply with a smaller request. A sociologic study conducted in the mid-1960s offers a stunning example of this "foot-in-the-door" technique. Sociologists went door to door asking homeowners to comply with a seemingly trivial request: to place a three-inch-by-three-inch card in the front window reading, "Be a Safe Driver." Two weeks later, researchers went back to those houses asking for permission to install an enormous and hideous billboard in the frontyard reading, "Drive Carefully." Just 17 percent of those who had refused to post the tiny cards in their windows agreed to the larger billboard request. Of those who had innocently made the initial commitment by posting the card, however, a whopping 76 percent agreed to allow the billboards to be installed in their frontyards. While petitions and endorsement cards can certainly persuade decision makers at city hall, their primary value is to help you get an initial, public commitment of support that can be used as a starting point for later, larger requests for assistance.

4. Ask for What You Want: While you used the "foot-in-the-door" approach to get the initial commitment, you use the "door-in-the-face" strategy when it comes time to actually turn out the troops for your approval hearing. With the DITF approach, you basically aim high and then settle for less if you have to. Open with a big request that you are prepared to have rejected ("Will you attend the hearing on Thursday evening and tell the council you support the expansion of the office park?"). If this large request is accepted, congratulations. If it's refused, then retreat to the smaller request you've had in your back pocket from the beginning ("If you can't attend the hearing, can you telephone the mayor and urge her to vote "yes" on the expansion?"). Starting with a high demand and then retreating to a smaller, more reasonable request will usually produce higher turnout than staking out an extreme position and refusing to back down gracefully.

5. Get a Decision to Act: It isn't enough to ask for what you want; you also have to give your supporter the emotional support he needs to turn pro-project attitudes into a decision to take pro-project action. What "hot buttons" do you need to hit to get your supporter to decide that he will, in fact, attend the hearing?

Goal Reinforcement: A citizen will agree to come to a hearing only when the ultimate outcome is desirable enough to make it worth the effort. Urging supporters to engage in personalized outcome visualization ("Picture yourself walking through the new town center") makes the benefits of your project more immediate and can inspire supporters to take action to make that vision a reality.

Consistency: Reminding your supporter that she already took an earlier pro-project position increases the likelihood that she'll sustain that position and agree to your request for more help: "We're asking people like you who signed our petition to . . .," or "You've been a longtime activist on affordable housing issues . . . ."

Easy Action: Supporters will be reluctant to undertake pro-project action that seems too troublesome, too time consuming, or too complex. You can make a daunting task such as "testifying at the Planning Commission hearing" seem more manageable by breaking it into smaller steps: driving to the county offices, parking the car, entering the hearing room, coming up to the microphone, and so on. Similarly, providing draft testimony or talking points to your supporters can be very helpful for people who are willing to speak up in favor of your project but can't figure out what to say. Just be certain that not all supporters will use the same talking points.

Peer Approval: A supporter will agree to help you only where he thinks he will gain some kind of social reward for doing so, or at least avoid being condemned by "everyone else." It is therefore crucial that supporters know that other people also like your project. In a classic series of studies about peer pressure, researchers found that participants were almost seven times more likely to take a minority position when they thought they had company than when they believed they would be the sole dissenter. The bottom line: make certain supporters know that other people share their enthusiasm for the project.

6. Encourage Actual Performance: It is much easier to *promise* to attend a hearing than it is to actually follow through on that pledge, and many developers end up waiting at City Hall for supporters who never show up. There are several ways you can increase the likelihood that an ally will actually perform as promised:

Process Simulation: A major reason why supporters don't do what they promise to do is that they don't make plans until the last minute. You can increase turnout by getting your supporters to consider the mechanics of performing the promised action in advance: "You'll probably have to leave work a little early in order to get to City Hall by 6:00 p.m. Once you get into the City Council chambers, you just walk up to the clerk at the front of the room and sign up to speak in favor of the project." By mentally rehearsing the promised event, the supporter can anticipate potential obstacles and distractions and be ready to deal with them when they arise.

Put It In Writing: Once you've gotten a supporter's promise to attend the hearing, put it in writing. Send a follow-up E-mail or letter confirming that your supporter is coming, reiterating the time and date of the hearing, and providing draft testimony or key messages. Putting your supporter's promise in black and white will make it much more likely that your ally will perform as promised.

Getting supporters to show up and testify on behalf of your project can be the most difficult and the most important part of a community involvement campaign. Numbers count. With a strategic approach and careful appreciation for some fundamental psychological principles, you can get the vocal citizen support you need at your next hearing.

CHECKLIST

✓ Keep everyone informed about the process through early and ongoing publicity.

✓ Disseminate basic information culled from studies that address likely concerns and project benefits.

✓ Select a convener, but stay constantly involved with important decision makers and intermittently involved with other participants at key points in the process.

✓ Determine the right combination of event types and their sequence.

✓ Enlist the help of capable professionals to manage meetings and presentations.

Part IV Communicating the What, Where, and When

Building a Communications Strategy

Having a communications plan in place will be important throughout whatever engagement process is selected. A well-constructed strategy will keep people informed, attract interest, and educate participants and the general public about the proposed project.

DEVELOPERS MAY RESENT THE TIME and trouble it takes to get the word out about the community engagement process—the constant reiteration of basic information about the whys and wherefores of a project. But to inform those out of the loop can amount to publicity and promotion of the project through inclusion and clarification; to update those already in the know can further engender or cement support for the proposed development. You will rely on communication tools of many types throughout the community engagement process. Skilled communications consultants can frame a worthwhile series of resources and events that will build toward a final plan. Communication tools are well known and widely used. They are intended to:

- Alert potential participants, public officials, and the general public about plans for launching a community engagement program regarding a proposed project;
- Inform potential participants, public officials, other community leaders, and the general public about the purposes and character of the proposed project;
- Attract broad participation in a scheduled series of events;
- Periodically let participants, public officials, and the general public know about progress in resolving key issues and reaching agreement about the proposed project;
- Remind participants about findings and conclusions from the previous event and the purposes and timing of the next event;
- Provide materials to allow participants to become better informed about the project and discuss it with others;
- Display posters, maps, plans, and designs in public places to attract the general public's attention to the project and the process.

To accomplish these aims, process organizers must plan to initiate a variety of communications strategies addressing all of the stakeholder audiences. Typical tools used to reach a broad audience in the community are described below.

In-House Published Information

A variety of published information can be generated in-house, in many cases inexpensively and without a great deal of extra effort. Clear, well-written reports or summaries, copies of studies available on request, eye-catching flyers, newsletters, E-mail alerts, and Web sites are commonly used, effective tools for conveying information about meetings, issues, and progress.

MANY FORMS OF COMMUNICATION can be crafted and issued by in-house staff and consultants to provide basic information about the project and how the engagement process is progressing. Often these are based on studies that few people will otherwise wade through, or notes on discussions that are not generally available.

Data Reports and Summaries

Information assembled by consultants and public planning staff provides factual data that is helpful in thinking through potential issues. Bear in mind, however, that it can be most helpful when the reports are readable summaries rather than impenetrably dry, long-winded accounts. The more straightforward and well-constructed the report, the better able the reader will be to educate himself and, at the same time, the more positive his experience of being involved in the decision making process. Summaries can be supplied as a matter of course as information becomes available, while complete studies can be offered upon request.

Flyers

One of the most frequently used communications vehicles is an information flyer that alerts potential participants and interested citizens to events in the community engagement process. Flyers are usually one- or two-page notices with catchy designs, intended to call attention to the process and tell people about its purpose and meeting times. Typically, they are printed in bulk for mailings, to pass out at meetings, and to aid in person-to-person conversations about the engagement process.

Newsletters

Especially if the process is lengthy—months or years—publication of periodic or occasional newsletters can keep recipients up to date on progress and event schedules. Formatting and printing newsletters is now easily done by computer and in-house printing equipment. Newsletters provide a means of getting the word out on program goals and accomplishments. They can be distributed to participants to record important findings and decisions, and to individuals, interest groups, and public officials not directly involved in the process but affected by the results. Regular publication of newsletters can keep current participants involved and attract new ones. Although newsletters should not be used to promote particular positions on issues, they can present pro and con arguments on issues still to be resolved, underscoring the open nature of the engagement process. In strongly polarized situations, it may be beneficial to form an advisory committee to review newsletter contents.

Electronic Media

Increasingly, people are using E-mail and Web sites to become and stay informed of current events. A roster of E-mail addresses should be compiled of members of key organizations involved in the community engagment process, including E-mail addresses obtained from participants in the initial events. Sending E-mail provides an easy and instant way to inform recipients about upcoming events, progress made, issues being examined, and other items of interest. Encouraging return E-mails, however, can generate a blizzard of messages that are time-consuming to answer and often provide an uneven flow of information. Also, there is no control over forwarding. Think carefully about the uses of E-mail and the capabilities for managing it.

Establishing a Web site for outreach processes has become commonplace. Web sites have become essential for providing not only news and progress reports, but for making reference materials and the latest sketch plans available as well. As the outreach program progresses, materials can be added to keep everyone current and provide valuable references to past actions.

Informative Events

You can't underestimate the value of putting a face to a name—or, in this case, putting a face to a project. Presentations with a personal touch are less formal and often highly instructive in the feedback they generate. Another approach, mounting exhibitions or displays, has the advantage of communicating the message in an ongoing way, providing a presence that conforms to passersby and their schedules.

PUTTING THE PEOPLE INVOLVED IN development and planning in front of the public helps to personalize the proposed project. Having them report publicly on why the project makes sense and how the discussions are proceeding infuses vitality into the process—a productive complement to printed information.

Briefings and Presentations

Briefings and presentations can inform elected officials, agencies, news media, and key interest groups about the community engagement process. They are especially useful in keeping public officials, who dislike surprises that might upset the political balance, knowledgeable about issues in play and decisions made. Generally, political briefings are most effective if arranged as informal meetings or phone calls rather than formal events. This allows for some give-and-take conversation about the status of the process, agenda changes, and other matters.

In addition, the initial survey of community leaders and interest groups should identify organizations that hold regular meetings or can arrange special meetings that provide opportunities for making presentations regarding the project and process. They may be civic or neighborhood groups, business associations, environmental organizations, or even religious groups. While such presentations must recognize the special interests of each group, they are tailor-made occasions for use of PowerPoint or slide presentations, for hands-on discussions of maps and preliminary plans, and for distributing newsletters and other printed information. Presentations also provide opportunities for obtaining follow-up comments and additional participation in the process.

Exhibits and Displays

Published materials and presentations can be supplemented by placing exhibits and displays in public places where many people otherwise unaware of the process can become familiar with it. Shopping malls, storefronts, courthouses, schools, or meeting places for important community events offer possibilities for mounting or erecting displays for a day or a week or even longer periods. Preparation of the materials may be expensive but worthwhile for extending the outreach effort to a wider audience. Exhibits and displays are even more effective if accompanied on occasion by knowledgeable staff who can initiate discussions about the proposals or other information portrayed.

Outside Publications

Is there anything better than good press? Simply put, cultivating good relationships with journalists will pay enormous dividends. Public service announcements in the press can be used to communicate basic information about an event, its time, and location. Advertisements can do the same with greater visibility, and also can be used to provide more substantive information or conduct surveys.

NEWS ABOUT THE PROJECT and the engagement process obtains wider circulation and frequently greater credibility when printed in a newspaper or local magazine or broadcast on a radio or television station. Although often difficult to arrange, friendly comments by the news media can be highly beneficial in gaining public support.

News Reports and Stories

Journalists may function as objective reporters and neutral observers but frequently are limited by their understanding of the events they are covering, by the time or space they are given to communicate information, and by pressures to heighten the news value of their findings. Still, it pays to establish friendly relations with media representatives; treat them with respect and let them observe the collaborative process at work. Assembling press kits with brief, basic information about the process will provide a useful reference. Press releases are more popular with organization staffs than with reporters, who are inundated with them daily. A better approach is to have a personal conversation with an editor or reporter that might suggest an angle on a story of particular interest to the public. Bringing selected participants together to chat with a journalist can make for an interesting story. Developers should be aware that reporters will look for and highlight newsworthy conflicts; however, careful interchanges with reporters can increase their understanding of the openness of the process, which in turn can lead to beneficial reporting of the results.

Public Service Announcements

Press releases are useful for placing public service announcements, which are sometimes available from news organizations. Brief notices of upcoming events, for example, along with complete information about time and location, can help to increase participation at important points in the process.

Advertisements

Paid advertisements of particularly important events, such as the initial information meeting, the final report on recommendations, or the dates of a multiday charrette, often can be arranged with local newspapers at little or no expense. Newspaper inserts can also be prepared to disseminate important information to many people in a community, and surveys are sometimes undertaken by including forms and mailing instructions in newspaper deliveries.

All the case study projects employed a battery of communications devices to widen the audience for the engagement process. The Eastern Cambridge planning project, for example, was operating in a hotbed of community and neighborhood activists, and used all the media available to keep people updated on what was going on. Most of the case studies employed some type of charrette, which can be an excellent showcase for elected officials, neighbors, and the news media about how community input is shaping the project planning process.

CHECKLIST

✓ Design a comprehensive communications strategy for the duration of the project.

✓ Consider making presentations yourself, or select a personable representative to put a "face" to the project.

✓ Determine where exhibitions or displays of the project might provide a positive presence.

✓ Find ways to engage the press in an effort to engender favorable coverage for the development.

Part V The Means of Participation

Tools for Engaging Participants

Numerous devices, ranging from the straightforward (a preliminary sketch pinned on a wall) to the complex (life-like computer-generated representations of project variables), are available to involve participants and elicit comments and approval.

LEADERS, MODERATORS, and facilitators of meetings use many tools to engage participants in fruitful discussion of development policies and projects. Some might fall under the heading of "tricks of the trade" for luring comments and ideas out of participants reluctant to speak. Asking provocative questions, asking for definitions of terms just introduced in the discussion, restating the immediate issue before the group, summarizing the ideas or concerns offered at some point, calling for greater definition of proposed approaches or solutions—all are methods that facilitators use to keep discussions going in productive ways.

Facilitators might use various voting methods to determine participants' preferences concerning the plan or design. This approach can be as simple as pinning a series of sketches showing alternative locations of proposed buildings on the wall and asking participants to provide a show of hands of which ones are most desirable. For more complex sketches or questions, participants can be given stickers to place their vote. Different colored stickers can be used to indicate high and low marks for various buildings or features. (This can also be done in small groups to stimulate discussion of the pros and cons of various plans and designs.)

Increasingly, more structured methods, many assisted by computer software, are being employed to elicit from groups the responses and comments that promote a shared understanding of issues, ideas, and possibilities. Some of the most popular help participants visualize building designs and project plans, or the effects of policies being considered. Some of the methods are copyrighted and available only through the consultants who invented them. But all seek to enrich the viewer's understanding of the visual effects of proposed policies and development plans.

The following headings begin with the simplest (and often least costly) approaches and progress to the more elaborate systems. Examples of resources for the materials or computer software required for some tools are listed as well. Don't assume that every tool is right for every situation, or that this selection represents a complete round-up of the tools available. *In addition, be aware that some of the more complex systems are primarily employed by corporations and government agencies for internal training, research, and planning purposes.*

Graphic Representation

A picture is worth a thousand words.

GRAPHIC REPRESENTATION tools include drawings, photographs, colored maps, aerial photographs, traffic flow diagrams, and any other types of drawings that present useful information. Many of these tools have been employed for generations to illustrate concepts and designs that are difficult to convey by words alone—the adage that one picture equals a thousand words still holds true. Hand-drawn drawings or sketches can suggest the qualities of finished development, sometimes with parts abstracted and enlarged to emphasize certain aspects of the design. Graphic portrayals of diagrams and tables can make complicated information easier to understand. Drawings, photos, diagrams, and tables are often inserted in slide presentations and, in addition, can be captured and manipulated by computer software as described below. Charrettes and other discussion formats that focus on site plan design issues usually generate dozens of quick sketches drawn during meetings, which can then be turned into more finished products as needed afterward.

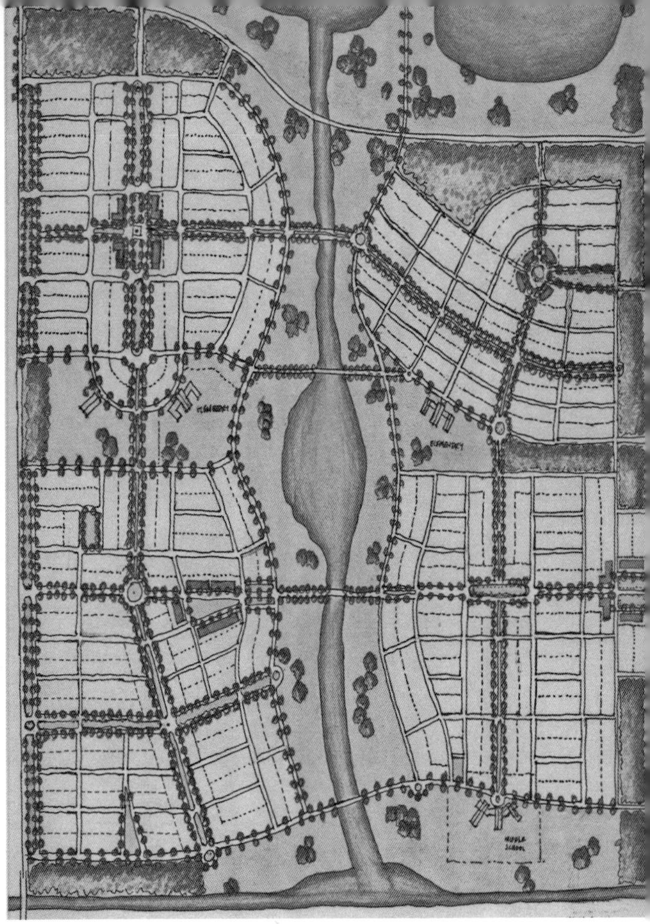

Once an overall plan is drawn up, sections can be enlarged for closer examination. This sketch of the North St. Lucie plan helped charrette participants understand how waterways that provide for drainage and conserve important ecosystems could also supply scenic settings for development.

This sketch of the central park proposed for Hellgate Meadows illustrated how the park would provide not only a pleasant space for recreation, but also an attractive setting for bordering commercial and service uses.

Three-Dimensional Models

Models can help people envision a project's relationship to its surroundings. Participants can even construct their own using basic materials, shifting elements around as needed to compare variables.

Going back to basics, participants can instead work on their own simplified model to picture the three-dimensional aspects of a project. In an interesting process known as "Box City," construction paper, cardboard boxes, glue, and markers are used to make a city block or street and show valued features and desirable changes.

During Crawford Square's planning phase, drawings illustrated how a mix of affordable and market-rate homes could form an attractive neighborhood.

FOR DECADES, THE WAY TO "sell" a project was by building a three-dimensional model to show buildings, streets, open spaces, landscaping details, and uses of surrounding parcels. Models show either the unadorned volume of buildings or add some architectural features. They make it easier for viewers to envision the relative sizes and volumes of buildings in relation to each other, streetscapes, and important visual features such as parks and sculptures. With some photographic skill, model photos can indicate at least rough ideas of streetscapes and prominent architectural features. However, once built, models can only be altered at considerable cost, and therefore present a static view of a finished product rather than an evolving plan.

To demonstrate how intensive new development could be meshed with the existing neighborhood around Volpe Center in Eastern Cambridge, a drawing was inserted (by use of Microsoft Photoshop) in an aerial photo of the area—another means of satisfying group interests in neighborhood design.

Group Mapping Exercies

Mapping exercises take the focus away from specific projects to a larger scale of development. Participants have a hand in determining where certain types of development should take place, after having considered the kinds of locational, environmental, and other concerns that must be addressed in mixed-use, large-scale development.

Source:

Box City
Ginny Graves, Center for Understanding the Built Environment (CUBE)
5328 W. 67th Street, Prairie Village, KS 66208
Telephone: (913) 262-0691
E-mail: ginny@cubekc.org
Web site: www.cubekc.org

Through a host of educational initiatives, CUBE teaches children the value of the built environment. CUBE's Box City process provides basic supplies for exercises in responsible citizenship and planning. Box City, created for young people, has crossed over for use in community groups and planning circles.

ORIENTED TO HANDS-ON planning at regional, community, and neighborhood scales rather than the design of specific projects, group mapping exercises allow participants to become involved in evaluating and recommending locations and areas for various types of development. The best-known example is the series of workshops organized for Envision Utah to map out a desirable future vision of regional growth. In the first workshop, participants were provided regional maps with a stack of chips scaled to represent the land area required to support a population increase of 1 million people at existing average suburban densities. The maps indicated existing developed areas and the environmental assets of the region. Participants placed chips where they thought development should occur, demonstrating their preference for development in infill or redevelopment sites. A second workshop used chips representing seven types of development, including three types of walkable communities, to be developed at a higher range of densities than the standard types of development. Again, participants placed the chips where they thought such development should occur and used markers to indicate open space and agricultural areas to be preserved. The results of the workshops were used to create two of the four future-growth scenarios evaluated in subsequent meetings.[1]

Mapping exercises are most helpful in exploring large-scale patterns of development. Developers of large-scale community projects may find them useful in introducing citizens to the kinds of locational, environmental, and other considerations that must be addressed in creating a mix of uses in a large site. Developers of smaller projects are more likely to choose a charrette type of process, which, in some respects, mirrors mapping exercises at a smaller scale.

Mapping exercises can be augmented by the use of some computer-assisted tools that allow users to create and evaluate regional or community scenarios. Generally, they require technical assistance to set up systems, input basic data, and guide planning choices and evaluations, but can provide almost instant feedback of scenario impact results.

Mapping exercises can include hands-on sketching of planning ideas.

Sources:

Community Viz
Orton Family Foundation
1035 Pearl Street, Boulder, CO 80302
Telephone: (303) 442-8800
Web site: www.communityviz.com

Three integrated components include Scenario Constructor, which lets users conduct impact analyses of development alternatives; Site Builder 3-D, which builds photo-realistic and interactive renderings of neighborhoods or projects that can be explored and visualized using virtual fly-through simulation; and Policy Simulator, which uses agent-based modeling to project the effects of planning policies.

Place3S
Nancy McKeever, Program Manager, California Energy Commission
MS-48, 1516 Ninth Street, Sacramento, CA 95814
Telephone: (916) 654-3948
Web site: www.energy.ca.gov/places

Place3S integrates public participation, community development and design, and computer-assisted quantification tools based on GIS to help communities evaluate plans for their effects on financial benefit, energy conservation, job growth and development, reduction of pollution, traffic congestion, and open space conservation.

Index
Criterion Planners/Engineers Inc.
725 NW Flanders Street, Suite 303, Portland, OR 97209-3539
Telephone: (503) 224-8606
E-mail: fino@crit.com
Web site: www.crit.com

Enables users to assess existing conditions and evaluate alternative plans. Indicators that assess existing conditions allow identification of problems and opportunities; users then construct, visualize, analyze, and compare alternative planning scenarios.

Quest
Envision Sustainability Tools, Inc.
1228 Hamilton Street, Vancouver, BC, Canada V6B 2S8
Telephone: (604) 225-2000
E-mail: info@envisiontools.com
Web site: www.envisiontools.com

Uses a computer gamelike interface to collaboratively explore the key challenges facing a region. Users make planning choices and can see their effects over 40 years.

What If?
78 Hickory Lane, Hudson, OH 44236-2707
Telephone: (330) 650-9807
E-mail: Info@What-if-PSS.com
Web site: www.what-if-pss.com

The GIS-based system lets users explore community development alternatives. Easy to use, it can be handled by nontechnical persons to project the impacts of policies on future land use patterns and on associated population, housing, and employment trends.

Keypad Polling

Using a keypad, participants can cast votes on issues and design alternatives and have the results instantly tallied. These devices can be most helpful where large numbers of people are weighing in, as in regional or citywide visioning or planning processes.

KEYPADS PROVIDED TO PARTICIPANTS in mapping exercises or other events involving multiple scenarios, priorities, or attributes, provide a means of gathering instant feedback in large-group settings. Keypads are linked into a network that allows instant voting on preferred aspects of alternatives and quick summations of the results. Polling firms use keypads with focus groups to test marketing presentations. Corporations use them for quickly evaluating a series of action items or business goals. For community engagement processes, polling can show the compiled ratings that participants give proposed building designs, types of uses, or densities in particular locations. Its capability for immediately assembling and summarizing responses to ideas being tested assists in reaching agreement on draft plans. Keypads are especially appropriate in situations where many participants are evaluating basic issues, as in regional or citywide visioning or planning processes. Multiple keypads and associated equipment are required. Keypads are also used extensively in computer-aided interactive discussions, which are described in a later section. For that reason, many firms that provide equipment and software for computer-aided discussions also offer keypad systems.

Sources:

Michael Smith, One Counts
4163 Fortuna Way, Suite B
Salt Lake City, UT 84124
Telephone: (801) 414-3073
Web site: www.onecounts.com

Provides keypads and software to support polling processes.

CoVision, Inc.
300 Brannan Street, Suite 408, San Francisco, CA 94107
Telephone: (415) 563-2020
Web site: www.covision.com

Employs keypads and multiple computers to enable the immediate tabulation and presentation of feedback from all participants in small and large group meetings.

(Both One Counts and CoVision are partners in America Speaks, which organizes and facilitates "town meetings" that allow citizens to participate in public decision making. Contact America Speaks at 1612 U Street, Suite 408, Washington, DC 20009; telephone (202) 299-1022; Web site www.americaspeaks.org.)

Meetingworks
4746 44th Ave., SW, Suite 100, Seattle, WA 98116
Telephone: (206) 467-1234
Web site: www.meetingworks.com

Provides products and services for electronic meeting and group decision support, including software and services.

GroupSystems
520 Zang Street, Suite 211, Broomfield, CO 80021
Telephone: (303) 468-8681
Web site: www.groupsystems.com

Offers technology, methodologies, and expert services to enable workgroups to improve decision making.

Image Surveys

Pairs of photographs are used to ask participants which version they like best. Results are then discussed with the group.

AN IMAGE SURVEY PRESENTS A SERIES of contrasting pairs of photographs showing streetscapes, types of buildings, parks, and other features of urban development. Participants are asked to identify the most desirable image in each pair. The result is tabulated and then discussed with the group. Contrasting images help participants to make distinctions between what they like and dislike, and the opinions of a large number of participants can give significant clues about the most desired forms of development. The comparative quality of the images is all-important, of course, and should not be used to "tilt" the voting.

Sources:

Anton Nelessen, Nelessen Associates
49 River Road, Belle Mead, NJ 08502
Telephone: (908) 431-0104
E-mail: vps@nelessen.org
Web site: www.nelessen.org

Uses paired photographs of built environments showing different physical conditions or simulated changes in conditions, shown to groups whose opinions are solicited through a survey.

Local Government Commission
1440 K Street, Suite 600,
Sacramento, CA 95814-3929
Telephone: (916) 448-1198
Web site: www.lgc.org

Contrasting images of the physical and natural conditions of a neighborhood are shown to groups, which are then asked about their preferences. LGC often works with local agencies to obtain images of local or regional development.

Looney Ricks Kiss
182 Nassau Street, Suite 201, Princeton, NJ 08542
Telephone: (609) 683-3600
Web site: www.lrk.com

Image surveys showing images of improvement options are distributed communitywide and responses indicate preferences.

The Local Government Commission in Sacramento shows pairs of photographs like these to determine citizen preferences for various designs of development—in this case, examples of single-family homes and retail centers.

Digital Photo Simulation

Variables can be inserted into the image of an existing site to show participants the "before and after."

DIGITAL IMAGES OF AN EXISTING streetscape or built environment can be modified to add proposed buildings, other design features such as street lights, trees, and grass medians, and transportation modes such as light rail lines, bus lanes, and pedestrian pathways. They work well as "before and after" comparisons and to show differences in alternative development designs. They can also be layered to illustrate incremental changes—adding a median strip, then street trees, then a building or two, etc. Although the tool is less compelling than the visualization tools described in the next section, it is significantly less expensive to produce.

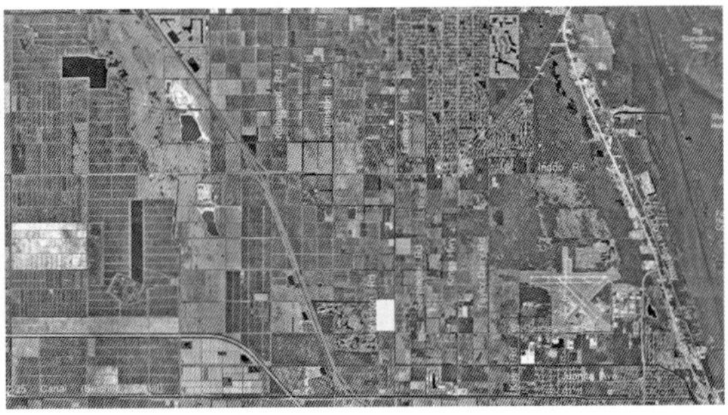

The consultant team for North St. Lucie County prepared a series of five digital photos to demonstrate how the planning area might develop over time without better planning for the future. These photos show existing conditions and a simulated version of what final buildout anticipated by 2025 might look like.

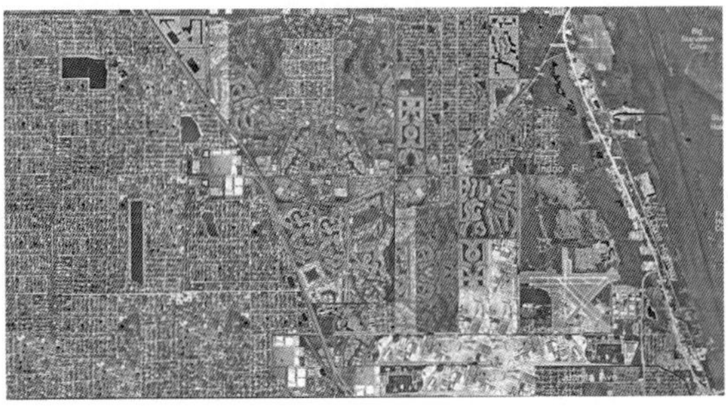

They work well as "before and after" comparisons and to show differences in alternative development designs.

Sources:

Richard Heapes, Street Works, LLC
30 Glenn Street, White Plains, NY 10603
Telephone: (914) 949-6505
Web site: www.street-works.com
Uses painting software to simulate the proposed development.

Steve Price, Urban Advantage
436 14th Street, Suite 1114, Oakland, CA 94612
Telephone: (510) 835-9420
Uses photo-editing software to add a proposed project to images of an existing site.

Ron Morgan, Urban Ventures
1900 Dilworth Road E, Charlotte, NC 28203
Telephone: (704) 342-2510
Web site: www.urban-ventures.com
Produces both aerial and street-level photographs to illustrate the effects of proposed projects.

Dover, Kohl & Partners
1571 Sunset Drive, Coral Gables, FL 33143
Telephone: (305) 666-0446
Web site: www.doverkohl.com
Illustrates phases of development and improvements for projects, neighborhoods, or corridors, building on photographs of existing conditions.

Winston Associates
4696 Broadway, Boulder, CO 80304
Telephone: (303) 440-9200
Uses three-dimensional visualization software to illustrate proposed developments.

Visualization Tools

A host of visualization software programs display realistic views, some with three-dimensional perspectives, of a project and its various alternatives.

VISUALIZATION IS INVALUABLE FOR understanding what proposed projects will actually look like, thus helping viewers to evaluate the impacts of policy and development options. Visualization software allows the display of realistic views of a project and alternatives. Depending on the software, the views may focus on only a predetermined number of perspective sketches or use Geographic Information Systems (GIS) capabilities to view a project from any perspective and to allow viewers to make and view changes. GIS-based visualization tools provide even more possibilities, allowing the choices made by participants to be incorporated and evaluated quickly, reducing the time required for gathering feedback. They even work fast enough to provide input into brainstorming exercises. Programs that provide animated three-dimensional views as if someone is walking or driving past a proposed development can be dazzling; even more sophisticated software can produce dynamic, multiple views from different locations to convey a clearer understanding of a project's visual character. In the North St. Lucie County charrette, specialists were brought in to prepare computer-generated animation of proposed designs for villages, towns, and higher-density urban development. They were able to show charrette participants how these areas might look as viewed from a car driving along a main street or from a plane flying overhead. Participants' reactions to the three-dimensional images told the consultant team that the higher-density urban designs were not found suitable for the area.

They were able to show charrette participants how these areas might look as viewed from a car driving along a main street or from a plane flying overhead.

Sources:

Autodesk, Inc.
111 Mcinnis Parkway, San Rafael, CA 94903
Telephone: (800) 551-1490 or (415) 507-5000
Web site: www.autodesk.com

Creates and animates detailed, realistic 3-D renderings, including light and shadow effects. Lets viewers visualize design alternatives from a set of predefined views, paths, and walk-throughs. No real-time interaction with viewers.

MultiGen-Paradigm, Inc.
550 S. Winchester Blvd., Suite 500, San Jose, CA 95128
Telephone: (214) 473-0256, Visual Simulation; (408) 965-0880, Urban Simulation
Web site: www.multigen.com

The "Creator" system enables real-time interaction and creates 3-D renderings. Users can "fly or walk" to any location and view details of the proposed built environment. Renderings are less detailed than in a non-real-time 3-D tool, but photographs of the project site can be used to make the views more realistic.

The "Site Builder" system allows users to quickly visualize spatial characteristics based on GIS information and "fly or walk" through a 3-D environment.

ESRI
380 New York Street, Redlands, CA 92373-8100
Telephone: (800) 447-9778 or (909) 793-2853
Web site: www.esri.com

The "3-D Analyst" system creates a 3-D terrain rendering of a place and a 3-D massing image of buildings from GIS information. The software has zooming and panning capabilities. 3-D Analyst is integrated into the ArcGIS Desktop and allows the creation of dynamic and interactive maps that elevate geographic visualization and analysis.

The ESRI "Model Builder" is an extension of ArcView Spatial Analyst software that lets users develop, share, and save spatial renderings.

Computer-Aided Interactive Discussions

Computer software can be used to display information on a large screen, readable by all participants in a room; it can enable interactive discussions among a number of locations; and it can facilitate electronic "town meetings" in which hundreds and even thousands of participants can be involved.

Computer software can be combined with keypad voting systems to record and provide fast feedback of participant proposals, thereby enabling interactive evaluations of development issues and building agreements on policies and designs. (Photo by Lenny Lind. Image used by permission from CoVision, Inc.)

COMPUTER SOFTWARE assists interactive discussions within meetings and allows interactive discussions among a number of discussion locations. Ideas and points can be recorded on a computer for visual display on a large screen readable by all the participants in a room. This can provide opportunities for revising and sharpening ideas and seeking a consensus on the results. The tool can be extended to be used in several locations at the same time and provide multiple inputs to a central point, with feedback to the various locations. This allows, for example, operation of a regional computer network involving a number of jurisdictions that can obtain and portray responses to proposals almost instantaneously. Most useful for community and regional visioning exercises, such electronic "town meetings" are expensive to mount but can attract the attention and involvement of hundreds and even thousands of participants.

CHECKLIST

✓ Think about which tools would most engage participants and generate results in your particular process.

✓ Which tools, while not strictly necessary, would greatly enhance the process? Check these against the budget.

Source:

CoVision, Inc.
300 Brannan Street, Suite 408, San Francisco, CA 94107
Telephone: (415) 563-2020
Web site: www.covision.com

Enables the immediate tabulation of feedback from all participants in large group meetings by using multiple computers.

(CoVision is a partner in America Speaks, which organizes and facilitates "town meetings" that allow citizens to participate in public decision making.)

America Speaks
1612 U Street, Suite 408, Washington, DC 20009
Telephone: (202) 299-1022
Web site: www.americaspeaks.org.

Meetingworks
4746 44th Ave., SW, Suite 100, Seattle, WA 98116
Telephone: (206) 467-1234
Web site: www.meetingworks.com

Provides products and services for electronic meeting and group decision support, including software and services.

GroupSystems
520 Zang Street, Suite 211, Broomfield, CO 80021
Telephone: (303) 468-8681
Web site: www.groupsystems.com

Offers technology, methodologies, and expert services to enable workgroups to improve decision making.

Endnotes
Parts I–V

PART I

1. Readers interested in further information about these concepts may wish to consult the following publications:

Smart growth: David O'Neill, *The Smart Growth Tool Kit* (Washington, D.C.: ULI, 2001); Douglas R. Porter, *Making Smart Growth Work* (Washington, D.C.: ULI, 2002).

Sustainable development: Douglas R. Porter, *The Practice of Sustainable Development* (Washington, D.C.: ULI, 2000); Judy Corbett and Michael Corbett, *Designing Sustainable Communities* (Washington, D.C.: Island Press, 2000).

Green building: *Green Developments* (CD prepared by the Rocky Mountain Institute with more than 200 case studies of green buildings throughout the world, 2001; available through ULI).

Neighborhood and town center designs: Charles C. Bohl, *Place Making: Developing Town Centers, Main Streets, and Urban Villages* (Washington, D.C.: ULI, 2002); Adrienne Schmitz, et al., *Creating Walkable Places: Compact, Mixed-Use Solutions* (Washington, D.C.: ULI, 2006).

Transit-oriented development: Robert Dunphy, et al., *Developing Around Transit* (Washington, D.C.: ULI, 2005).

Green infrastructure systems: Alexander Garvin, *Parks, Recreation, and Open Space*. American Planning Association, PAS 497/498, 2001; Randall G. Arendt, *Conservation Design for Subdivisions: A Practical Guide to Creating Open Space Networks* (Washington, D.C., Island Press, 1996).

2. Michael Thomsett, *NIMBYism: Navigating the Politics of Local Opposition* (Arlington, Virginia: Centerline Publishing, 2004).

PART II

1. Dwight H. Merriam, *The Complete Guide to Zoning* (New York: McGraw-Hill, 2005), p. 119.

2. Ibid., p. 116.

PART III

1. Adapted from Susan L. Carpenter, *Solving Community Problems by Consensus* (Washington, D.C.: Program for Community Problem Solving, 1990), p. 33.

2. Author telephone interview with Bill Lennertz, National Charrette Institute, November 4, 2004.

3. Debra Stein, "Charrettes: Not Always the Right Answer," *Land Development*, Winter, 2001.

4. Drawn from the Web site of the National Charrette Institute: www.charretteinstitute.org.

5. Dwight H. Merriam, *The Complete Guide to Zoning* (New York: McGraw-Hill, 2004), p. 120.

PART V

1. Peter Calthorpe and William Fulton, *The Regional City* (Washington, D.C.: Island Press, 2003), pp. 126–129.

Part VI

Case Studies of Community Engagement Processes for Planning and Development

Seven case studies were prepared to illustrate the purposes, procedures, and tools of community engagement processes. The studies represent a variety of geographic settings, sponsorships, central issues, and approaches to reaching agreement on plans for urban development projects and plans. The community engagement processes, all of which were successful in these places, employed many of the techniques and tools discussed in the prior sections.

Case Study
Crawford Square, Pittsburgh, Pennsylvania

The developer joined with a city agency and community development group to sponsor a citizens' engagement process in an area where resident attitudes toward development had long been hostile. Involving a series of public and small-group meetings and a charrette, it resulted in agreement on a development plan for an inner-city redevelopment area.

THE SETTING

The city of Pittsburgh has been reviving failed neighborhoods for decades, bringing the powers of its redevelopment authority to bear on property acquisition, then working with community groups and developers to design and build new inner-city neighborhoods. It has been a long road, fraught with disputes and disappointments. But especially in the past decade or two the city has completed several residential renewal projects that have won national attention.

One especially successful development is Crawford Square, a mixed-income residential development on 17.5 acres in the lower Hill District on the east side of downtown. The redevelopment agency brought in a St. Louis development company, McCormack Baron Salazar, a firm well recognized for its successful construction of mixed-income housing projects in many cities, to coordinate planning and to manage construction and operation of the development. A firm that customarily establishes close relationships with local community groups, McCormack Baron Salazar formed a joint venture with the Hill Community Development Corporation, the Hill Project Area Committee, and the Urban Redevelopment Authority. It then engaged members of these organizations in a community outreach process to make key planning and design decisions about redevelopment of the area. This developer-led process included a variety of public meetings, a charrette, and intensive small-group meetings with members of the project area committee.

ESTABLISHING A POSITIVE DEVELOPMENT CLIMATE

The first order of business for developer McCormack Baron Salazar was to create a positive environment for planning and development in the Hill District. Hill residents had a deep distrust of the redevelopment authority. Once a thriving community known for its jazz clubs (Oscar Peterson and Cannonball Adderly, among others, entertained in the Hill District), the neighborhood fell on hard times in the postwar years. In the 1950s, the redevelopment authority targeted the area for urban renewal and, over five years, uprooted 8,000 residents to make room for civic cultural development. Angry citizens staged a dramatic march

The neighborhood had been all but wiped out over years of demolition and neglect.

on the redevelopment agency, putting an end to the urban renewal that had failed them utterly. The neighborhood suffered further damage during the 1968 riots following the assassination of Dr. Martin Luther King.

Desultory redevelopment during ensuing years resulted in a patchwork of small projects, too insignificant in their impact to appreciably reverse or ameliorate the blight. The Hill Community Development Corporation was launched in 1987 to help restore the community's social and economic fabric, but it found the redevelopment process difficult and contentious.

It is not surprising, then, that the redevelopment authority was met with suspicion about its motives when it returned to the Hill in the late 1980s to assemble property for the Crawford Square project. The neighborhood still contained the highest concentration of low-income housing in the city. Previous plans for the area prepared over the years had proposed to expand downtown-style development into the neighborhood, leading inner-city residents to believe that the city's primary redevelopment objective was wholesale "Negro removal." Even in the 1990s, longtime residents continued to doubt the Authority's motives. Added to these fears was a split in neighborhood views about the future character of residential redevelopment. Some saw attraction of higher-income households as the answer; others preferred a focus on low-cost housing.

Through decades of work in redeveloping inner-city neighborhoods, McCormack Baron Salazar had configured a planning and development model that it has used successfully in many cities. The firm develops a mix of market-rate and subsidized housing and employs planning and design methods that are sensitive to local concerns and needs, that involve local citizens in decisions, and that incorporate facilities and services that add to the social and economic life of the area. The developer's approach to launching the Crawford Square project began with the formation of the joint venture with the redevelopment agency—the nominal client—but also with a community-based organization and a project committee.

Membership in the Crawford Redevelopment Committee was determined by the three principals involved—the redevelopment agency, the developer, and the community development corporation. Structured to involve the many interests concerned with the area's redevelopment, it included representatives of community groups, civic activists, local residents, city officials, and business interests. The area's city councilman also sat in on most meetings. It was hoped that stimulating an open exchange of ideas and opinions among these committee members would lead to a consensus on a plan.

The developer signed up a well-known Pittsburgh architectural firm, Urban Development Associates (UDA), as the principal consultant for preparing the plan. Besides wide experience in designing many types of projects across the nation, UDA had worked on a number of redevelopment efforts in Pittsburgh. It knew the city and the neighborhood. It also had a track record of working with local citizens to formulate plans.

THE PROCESS

Before initiating discussions with the committee, the developer and consultants interviewed a number of community leaders about their concerns vis-à-vis future development, and identified other members of the community whose opinions on a new plan would be important to gaining a consensus. A number of committee members also toured several of the developer's projects in other cities to hear favorable accounts firsthand from their residents. As a tool for assisting discussions, UDA expanded a three-dimensional model of downtown it had prepared for another assignment to include the Hill District, showing the existing buildings and streets at the site and in the surrounding area.

The first meeting with the committee occurred in the U.S. Steel Building in downtown Pittsburgh, in a room dozens of stories above the street. The views down into the neighborhood emphasized the proximity of the project area to downtown—a mere five-minute walk. The model was also brought in. The group was coached by the UDA facilitator to consider two questions about members' perceptions of the site: What kind of development should occur in this area? And what concerns and problems will affect what and how redevelopment takes place? The intent was to move the group past feelings of apprehension and distrust to positive considerations about what could happen in the Hill District.

In this meeting and others, participants had no inhibitions about commenting on plans and making suggestions. Ray Gindroz of UDA remembers that one visitor occasionally took to fuming over the area's disastrous history, but those moments waned as the committee continued to dig into the real question of what the neighborhood should become. As the plan took shape, committee members took heart in the project's potential.

Two guiding principles emerged early in the process:

- Crawford Square should look as little like a "project" and as much like a traditional Pittsburgh neighborhood as possible;
- Housing should provide for different types of households and be available for rental and sale.

UDA conducted surveys to determine the defining characteristics of existing East End neighborhoods that could be incorporated in the design of Crawford Square. Based on this information and comments made at the first meeting, UDA began working out initial design criteria and conducting analyses of key elements—street systems, open space, relationships to nearby development, etc. A series of meetings at the redevelopment authority offices, some smaller in order to examine particular issues, began to move from concepts to design details. UDA organized what Gindroz now calls a "hybrid" charrette, only three days long and held at the firm's offices downtown near the site. (Gindroz remarks, "The early 1990s were early days in the charrette business, when we didn't have a set structure for these processes. Now we have a much more detailed idea of the sequence and kinds of events we undertake.") At two major community meetings, UDA presented the findings of the site analysis and a first attempt at defining design guidelines. The guidelines were the subject of discussion by breakout groups, and their reports fed into the later finalization of the design.

The new Crawford Square—an inner-city neighborhood reconstituted with a mix of affordable and market-rate housing along pleasant streets.

Much time was spent trying out a variety of building designs. The committee wished to add diversity in housing types to accommodate differing family structures, but it was also concerned that the various types appear related in basic design. In the end, all the different housing types—rental and for-sale, detached and attached, one-, two-, and three-bedroom units—were designed as traditional housing common in East End neighborhoods, eliminating design features often associated with low-income "projects." The homes feature tall, narrow windows, bay windows, dormers, and gable ends facing the street. Many façades are made of brick and have porches. Houses and apartments are two and three stories high.

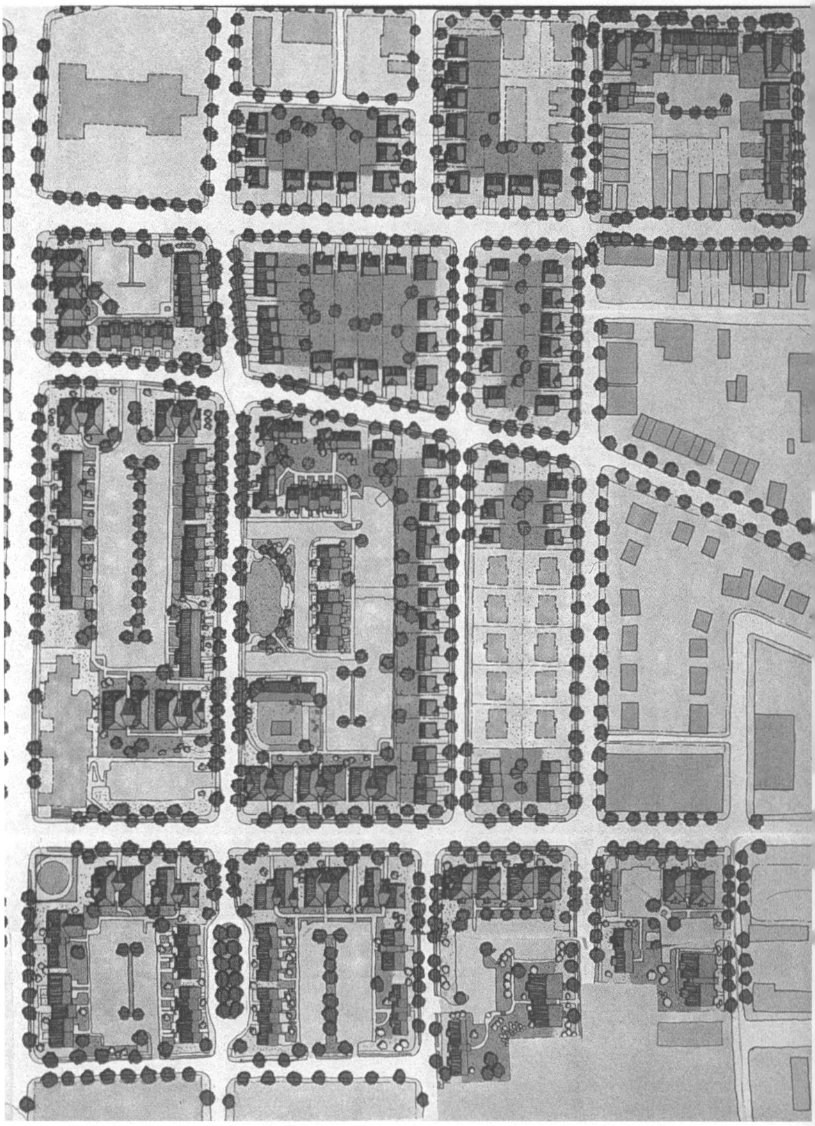

In a series of working sessions with neighborhood and community leaders, site designers integrated new residential development with preserved homes and other structures, all based on the existing street system.

THE PLAN

The plan came together within a six-month period of twice-a-week meetings. The layout appears rather simple but fits into the city's fabric and meets community goals for creating a traditional neighborhood. Housing is oriented within a gridiron street pattern, extending that of the surrounding residential areas. Sidewalks and planting strips with attractive lighting border each street. All buildings are set back 20 to 25 feet to create front yards. The steep 15-percent slope of the site precluded development of alleys and rear-loaded garages found in a traditional neighborhood. Instead, single-family houses have garages located beneath the front porch, hidden from the street. Apartment buildings and townhomes are served by gated parking spaces in the interior of each block. On-street parking is allowed. Three small parks were constructed and other amenities include a swimming pool, a community center, and a fitness center. The overall density of development is 22 units per net acre and 16 units per gross acre.

Gindroz estimates that the community engagement process was budgeted at about $75,000, with another $125,000 or so spent on services required to produce a finished plan. He points out that the cost numbers are 14 years old and therefore would be higher today.

THE OUTCOME

Construction of 409 housing units was carried out in three phases, completed in 1993, 1995, and 1999. Each of the phases included a mix of rental and for-sale units. Combined, the development includes 349 rental units and 60 for-sale townhouses and detached homes. After the first phase, McCormack Baron Salazar supported the Hill District Community Development Corporation as the lead organization for developing for-sale units. When the market for for-sale housing proved stronger than expected, the number of apartment units was reduced to allow more development of single-family homes.

All told, about 800 residents live in Crawford Square. Over 500 live in rental units, of which 56 percent are rented to households at income levels below 60 percent of the regional median income. Market-rate units rented for $745 per month for a one-bedroom unit to $1,245 per month for a three-bedroom unit. For-sale units initially sold in the range of $80,000 to $120,000, but in the final phase were priced at $90,000 to $300,000.

The success of Crawford Square has energized the market in the Hill District: two small retail centers have opened in the area; the CDC has built other subsidized hous-ing nearby; a HOPE VI project is underway; and two new office buildings have been constructed in the area. Where razing the vital features of community in the name of urban renewal once sapped the Hill's lifeblood, responsible, inclusive development has restored it back to health.

References:

Author's telephone interviews with Vincent Bennett, project manager for McCormack Baron Salazar, February 1, 2005; and with Ray Gindroz of UDA, February 2, 2005.

Profiles on the Crawford Square development prepared by McCormack Baron Salazar (undated), UDA (undated), the Urban Redevelopment Authority of Pittsburgh (undated), the Urban Land Institute, 1999, and the *Affordable Housing Design Advisor,* 2002.

Deitrick, Sabina and Cliff Ellis. "New Urbanism in the Inner City: A Case Study of Pittsburgh." *Journal of the American Planning* Association, Vol. 70, No. 4 (Autumn, 2004): pp. 426–433.

Jones, Tom, William Pettus, and Michael Pyatok. *Good Neighbors: Affordable Family Housing.* New York: McGraw-Hill, 1995. Pp. 24, 168–171.

Case Study

Eastern Cambridge Planning Study, Cambridge, Massachusetts

The city sponsored a citizen-based planning process to determine the amount and character of private development in a rapidly growing infill and redevelopment area. Intensive discussions with a citizens' group—once opposed to new development—plus public meetings and workshops created a plan that provided a springboard for development activity.

The Eastern Cambridge Planning Study was commissioned by the city of Cambridge to provide a planning framework for a substantial increase in private development in the area. A consultant team was employed to work with a citizens' advisory committee to make recommendations regarding the amount and character of future development. Through an intensive series of large and small discussions, the committee learned about the dynamic functions and character of the community and came to a consensus on major policy decisions as well as detailed design approaches. Their recommendations were adopted by the city council and have guided significant development taking place in Eastern Cambridge.

THE SETTING

Sustained economic growth in the city of Cambridge has increased the pressure for new development. New citywide growth management policies and rezoning adopted in 1997 and 2001, respectively, attempted to place tighter controls over the amount and character of that development, but neighborhood residents were still anxious. Eight major development projects had been initiated in Eastern Cambridge in the late 1990s, adding more than 2.5 million square feet of building space, most of it for office and R&D uses. Moreover, market projections predicted about nine million square feet of residential and commercial development allowed by existing zoning in Eastern Cambridge by 2020. Given this growth trend, citizens feared the encroachment of commercial development into residential areas, increasing traffic congestion, real estate price escalation, and the inadequacy of public open space to serve new development.

Neighborhood residents petitioned the city council to request an 18-month moratorium on major projects until a study could recommend appropriate policies and zoning to guide development in the area. Many assumed that the subtext of the petition was to block 12 million square feet of new development allowed by current zoning. The council established the moratorium in January 2000, and an 18-member Eastern Cambridge Planning

Study Committee (ECaPS) was appointed to oversee the study, working with a multidisciplinary consultant team led by Goody Clancy, a Boston architectural and planning firm.

The ECaPS committee, appointed by the city manager, included the person who had initiated the petition, other residents and property owners, developers, local business representatives, and city staff. They had 18 months to understand the dynamics of this active living and working area, resolve development issues, agree on an overall plan, and make recommendations about appropriate zoning.

STUDY AREA CHARACTERISTICS

The study area lies in the northeast corner of the city, south of its border with Somerville and reaching to the Charles River on the east, where it becomes a major gateway from downtown Boston to Cambridge. Its character derives from its industrial past and the diversity of the four neighborhoods in the area. In the early 1800s, the area's proximity to Boston and cheap immigrant labor attracted many types of industries, along with worker housing. By the mid-20th century, the decline in manufacturing had left many industrial buildings vacant, a substantial number of which were razed by urban renewal programs to make way for new office development. In the 1980s, a research-based economic boom stimulated in part by proximity to the Massachusetts Institute of Technology accelerated the pace of development, leading to a dramatic increase in construction of office and research buildings. In addition, a mix of new development and redevelopment in former industrial areas added substantial numbers of housing units to the area, although not enough to keep up with demand. Today, Eastern Cambridge combines the ambience of historic, mixed-income, tightly knit neighborhoods with a mix of commercial and office buildings, some quite substantial in size and bulk.

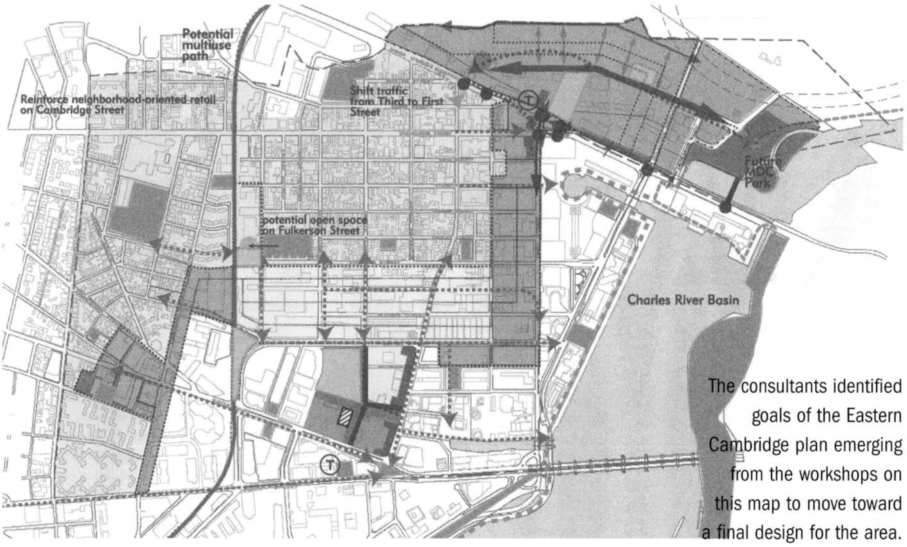

The consultants identified goals of the Eastern Cambridge plan emerging from the workshops on this map to move toward a final design for the area.

For the purposes of the study, six distinctive areas were delineated:

- Kendall Square, the location of the Volpe Center and other office and R&D uses;
- East Cambridge, one of the oldest residential neighborhoods in the area;
- The Transition Area between them, characterized by commercial and industrial development in a variety of scales;
- North Point, isolated by highways, rail yards, and water but with plenty of open land;
- The Wellington/Harrington neighborhood, mostly residential except near Kendall Square;
- Area IV, with traditional one- and two-family homes and public housing developments with some office development.

The site analysis conducted by Goody Clancy identified key themes based on existing development patterns and potential opportunities to help guide the design of future development:

- The historic block pattern creates a walkable, pedestrian-scale environment, emphasizing the importance of connectivity between existing street grids and pedestrian pathways as a useful model for future development;
- Well-defined street walls, human-scale buildings, and windows at street level are essential to creating an attractive pedestrian environment;
- Introducing gradual changes in building scale and massing in the area between residential neighborhoods and the commercial development around Kendall Square would help achieve compatibility between these areas;

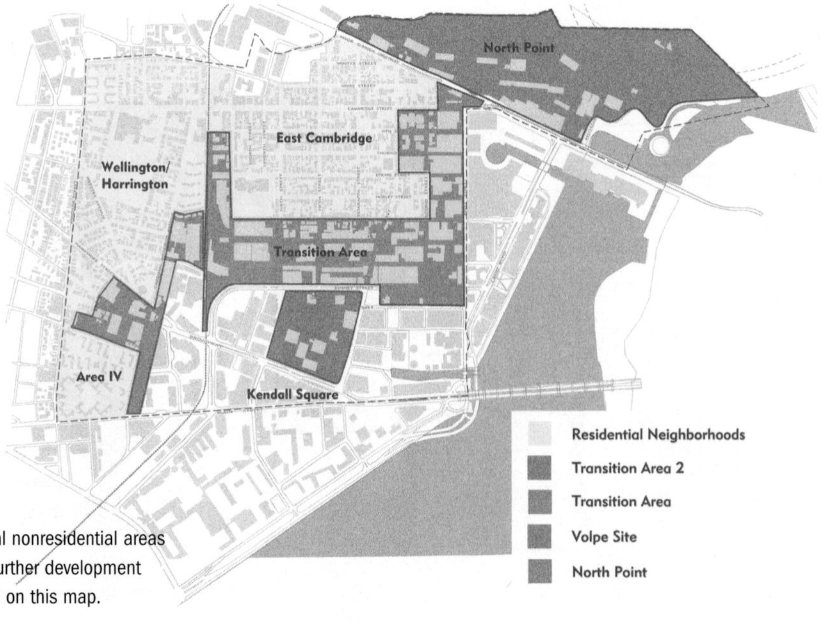

The principal nonresidential areas subject to further development are outlined on this map.

- Well-designed civic buildings such as the Bulfinch Courthouse on Cambridge Street play a key role in the image and identity of existing neighborhoods that should be carried over to new development areas where possible;
- Open space located adjacent to other community facilities creates a strong interaction between uses that supports community life;
- A critical mass of street-level retail creates lively commercial districts that should be encouraged where appropriate.

These observations set the stage for engaging the issues to be resolved during the study process.

THE PROCESS

Following an intense study of existing conditions, the consultant team began meeting with the ECaPS committee in June 2000, at first every week and eventually two or three times a week. David Dixon, Goody Clancy's project manager, says the first job was education, especially to dispel a lot of myths. For example, traffic congestion, always a concern, could be understood by tracing how traffic worked in Eastern Cambridge (and discovering that most traffic was passing through the area, not originating there); tall buildings were considered obnoxious but might be appropriate in certain areas where they would not overshadow neighborhoods. The committee spent a considerable amount of time discussing the real meaning of density in terms of community interaction and walkability, and understanding how small parks may be more attractive and useful than large parks.

The committee evolved a stance that its primary purpose was not to "protect" neighborhoods, but how to leverage development to enhance neighborhoods. Growth, in other words, could be harnessed to accomplish useful ends.

During this period, the ECaPS committee sponsored its first public meeting, on September 27, 2000. Largely an informational meeting, the event drew about 80 participants who learned about the makeup of the committee, how the study was being conducted, and how they could participate in future events.

From a concentration on problems and issues, the committee moved to fashioning a vision of the future of Eastern Cambridge. What should it look like? How should it function as a community? What services were needed? What can be done to reduce street traffic? The answers to these questions began to form a picture of tomorrow's Eastern Cambridge as a mixed-use, compact, walkable, and livable place. The committee was aided in this process by the organization of the first charrette, centered on creating a vision and held on a Friday evening and Saturday in late October. About 75 people attended, including city councilors, state representatives, planning board members, and neighborhood residents, in addition to committee members. Friday night, after a quick dinner and conversations, the consultant team presented the results of interviews with key community stakeholders, described area trends in transportation and real estate development, explained affordable housing and public realm issues, and spelled out initial committee goals. Then attendees were given opportunities to circulate among briefing tables to learn more and provide input; they moved every half hour to another table, thus engaging three issues.

On Saturday morning (breakfast and lunch included), about the same number of people arrived, with two-thirds having participated the day before. Informal discussions led to a review of what the group had learned the previous evening. (At this point, an open space advocate tried to dominate the discussion but was resisted by the majority of participants who said they wanted to move ahead to work on visions for Eastern Cambridge.) For the next three hours, participants divided into five work groups to prepare a broad set of goals for development in Eastern Cambridge and to describe a conceptual vision for each of the major areas defined by ECaPS. Each group included committee members and city staff as well as a prearranged mix of neighborhood advocates, developers, property owners, and others. At least two consultant team members worked with each group. When the groups reported their results, says Dixon, "It was remarkable that neighborhoods that had spent years fighting development articulated, for the first time, goals for the kinds of development—uses, scale, design character, traffic characteristics—they would like to see occur in Eastern Cambridge."

Dixon gives credit to the educational workshops on Friday night, where people had an opportunity to discuss issues interactively, and the intermixing of multi-stakeholder vision groups on Saturday, which brought people together to focus on sharing a vision. In both instances, the setting allowed for asking questions and probing for answers in real time. The charrette definitely signaled to participants—and the city—that collectively they held more complex and nuanced views about development in Eastern Cambridge than had been anticipated. They were ready, says Dixon, for an in-depth process to identify the type and amount of development that was appropriate.

While the consultants continued to meet with the ECaPS committee, another charrette, this one focused on urban design, was set for Saturday, December 2. Roughly 100 people par-

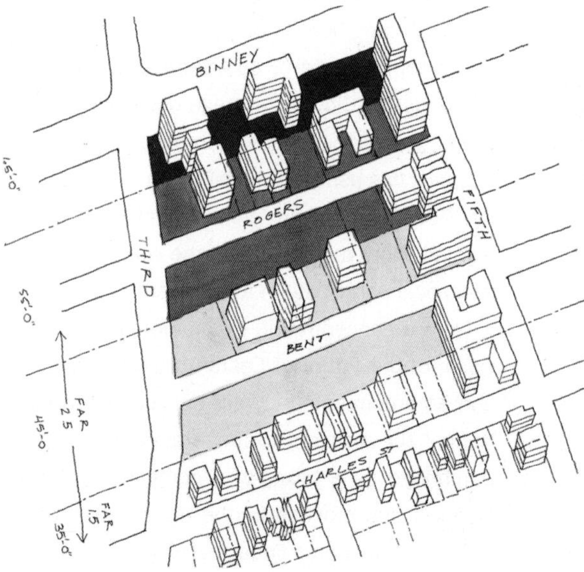

In response to residents' concerns, the plan calls for encouraging residential uses in the Transition Area through a zoning overlay and for a transition of building heights from the neighborhoods to higher-density development around Kendall Square.

ticipated, about half of whom had been involved in the first charrette. After reviewing the results of the first charrette, four work groups were formed, including a mix of participants similar to those formed for the first charrette. Each of the groups was asked to focus on one of the four development areas that, combined, could accommodate about 90 percent of anticipated growth. The task was to prepare a list of goals and guidelines and design a physical vision for the assigned area. The groups were given Styrofoam blocks cut to represent one-, three-, five, and ten-story housing, office, research, and other types of buildings. Green paper could become parks and gray paper could be used for new streets.

Three hours later, the groups reported and discussed their conclusions. Goals for North Point, for example, included creating a new mixed-use district with strong visual and pedestrian connections to East Cambridge, and building new streets to improve connections to adjoining neighborhoods. Examples of goals for the Volpe Block included creation of a major new public park surrounded by residential and retail uses. In general, the groups supported significant development where it would make sense—near transit stations, filling in gaps along main streets to improve walkability, putting residents around a lively new park. The groups recommended building heights ranging from three stories next to traditional neighborhoods to 25 or more stories next to transit stations. With the exception of one participant who wanted much more green space than did others, people recommended appropriately sized and located parks.

At one of the workshops, members of the advisory group planned where various types of development, represented by Styrofoam blocks, should be located.

The committee continued to meet following these charrettes and was able to transmit zoning recommendations to the planning board in April 2001, which provided time for discussion prior to the expiration of the 18-month moratorium. Subsequently, the committee met in four working sessions in April through August to review zoning recommendations and finalize design guidelines—sessions that Dixon calls some of the most productive in the process, symbolizing the significant stake of committee members in the outcome. The planning board completed rezoning decisions and submitted them to the city council in June 2001; they were adopted in October.

As the participants

"examined the issue of density, they figured out that less development would be less good."

During the process, three newsletters were published to describe ongoing progress, and a bulletin explaining the proposed rezoning was widely circulated. In addition, the consultant team provided updates to businesses at meetings of the Cambridge Chamber of Commerce and the Cambridge Street Business Association.

THE PLAN

Given the initial attitude of many Eastern Cambridge residents that development should be reined in, the plan they developed proposes very modest reductions in zoning allowances for future development. Under the citywide rezoning proposal, market projections for the next 20 years had anticipated development of about 7.8 million square feet of new building space, with a significantly larger component of residential space than existing zoning would have allowed. By comparison, the new plan projects development of 7.3 million square feet of space over the next 20 years, with a slightly higher proportion of residential development. The willingness of Eastern Cambridge residents to accept this scale of future development comes as a direct result of their participation in evaluating land use options and understanding how new development could be accommodated without destroying their quality of life.

During the study period, residents began to recognize the opportunities presented by future development in Eastern Cambridge, including:

- Significant amounts of residential development and new neighborhoods in the North Point and Volpe Center areas previously dominated by industrial and commercial uses;
- Substantial amounts of affordable housing as part of the large-scale development of residential areas;
- New residential "rooftops" that permit additional retail development, helping to create lively and pedestrian-friendly neighborhoods;
- New development and redevelopment providing opportunities to create transitions in height and uses between low-scale residential neighborhoods and higher-scale development around Kendall Square and along the riverfront.

This drawing evokes the proposed character of substantial mixed-use development along Third Street to create a pedestrian-friendly connection between Kendall Square and the nearby residential neighborhood.

As Dixon puts it, "As the participants examined the issue of density, they figured out that less development would be less good." That is, development would form the lively main streets and create the connections between neighborhoods. A halt in development would leave opportunities on the table. In particular, the committee found the prospect of developing over 4,400 housing units in the area, including sizeable amounts of affordable housing, highly satisfying. These ideas became the core of the plan.

The plan presented an overall vision for Eastern Cambridge (e.g., "Promote land use patterns that improve quality of life in residential neighborhoods and foster a vital public realm in mixed-use districts") and sets of goals for urban design, open space, land use and density, housing, economic development, and transportation, all illustrated by photographs of existing buildings and streets. Zoning recommendations built on this conceptual foundation. For each of the six areas, a diagrammatic map identifies major recommendations (parks, pedestrian paths, building forms, connections to adjoining areas), a site plan illustrates the form and scale of the built environment, and a series of "before and after" photos and drawings illustrate development opportunities in important locations.

In addition, non-zoning recommendations pertained to open space, transportation, non-auto mobility, a retail strategy, and noise impacts of development. Transportation issues were difficult to address. The goal of reducing by half the new car trips that existing zoning would have generated proved elusive. The planned land use scenario that will encourage walking, biking, and transit use, supplemented by a 20 percent reduction in required parking, would lower overall auto trips by an estimated 20 percent. To reach the desired 50 percent reduction in auto trips will require aggressive implementation of travel demand management programs and improvements in transit accessibility (planned but uncertain).

During the final four months of the committee's work, the consultant team also drew up design guidelines addressing the built form of development—the use, scale, and character of buildings—and the public realm—the connections, streets and sidewalks, open spaces, and transportation system. The guidelines are intended to guide planning board decisions on special permit applications for projects in the study area.

THE OUTCOME

After approval of the study committee's recommendations for rezoning and the end of the moratorium, development has surged in Eastern Cambridge. In a three-year period, 5.2 million square feet of new building space have been approved in North Point, including 2.2 million square feet of office and R & D space, some retail space, and 2,400 to 2,700 dwelling units. In the Volpe block, 527 housing units with accessory retail shops are being constructed along Third Street, 211 housing units and 9,700 square feet of retail space are under development along First Street, and a candy factory has been adapted for use as housing with ground-floor retail. The plan has been successful in preparing the way for development that will improve neighborhood and economic conditions. Residents and developers know what to expect.

References:

Author's telephone interviews with David Dixon of Goody Clancy, January 17, February 3, and June 8, 2005.

Eastern Cambridge Planning study. Prepared by the Cambridge Community Development Department and the Eastern Cambridge Planning Study Committee for the City of Cambridge, October 2001.

Case Study
Hellgate Meadows, Missoula, Montana

The developer commissioned a charrette to help plan a traditional neighborhood design (TND) for a town center and adjoining residential areas. The open charrette process generated strong public support for the innovative design, enabling the developer to accommodate a mix of uses and win timely approval of a TND ordinance needed for the project to move forward.

Hellgate Meadows, a neotraditional, mixed-use development in Missoula, Montana, was planned through a community outreach process sponsored by a locally based developer, Bob Brugh, of Neighborhoods by Design, LLC. Although he had previously focused on big-box retail development, Brugh proposed two innovative approaches to planning his next project: a design modeled after the traditional neighborhood design concept, and community participation in the design process. As of early 2005, two-thirds of the town center land had been sold, much of the retail and mixed-use section of the town center had been completed, and more than 322 residential units of various types had been built and sold or rented.

THE SETTING

Missoula lies near the western border of Montana with Idaho, at the fork of the Clark Fork and Bitterroot rivers. It is a university town and a regional headquarters for the U.S. Forest Service, and hosts a great many tourists coming through to reach Glacier National Park, three hours to the north, and Yellowstone National Park, three-and-a-half hours to the east. Surrounded by national forests and a handful of wilderness areas, the Chamber of Commerce Web site assures us Missoula is "not a bad place to hang out in the summer or (if you like the snow) the winter." The growing city population, up from 43,000 in 1990 to 57,000 in 2000, attests to its livability.

Missoula is also the center of retail trade for a wide area—the Chamber of Commerce claims ten counties. Bob Brugh, the sponsor of the recent charrette, honed his skills by managing development of a 1.1 million-square-foot retail power center in Missoula that includes a Costco store, Target, Home Depot, an Albertsons grocery store, Barnes & Noble, Office Depot, Petsmart, and a variety of other retail outlets—all within a quarter mile or so from the mixed-use site he is now interested in developing. In fact, Brugh's interest in developing a town center arose in large part from the clamor of potential clients for additional retail and service building sites. Without a doubt, retailing is an important economic driver in Missoula.

"Hellgate" seems an inauspicious name for a development project, but the term is historic. French trappers found the carnage of war in a canyon outside of town, apparently the result of battles between Indian tribes. The name was applied to the beginnings of a town and the first trading post which eventually became Missoula. Hellgate Meadows harkens back to the early days of the city, and Brugh's intent was to reproduce some of the design approaches found in Missoula's older neighborhoods.

THE PROJECT IN PRELIMINARY FORM

In late 1997, when the commercial project was nearly sold out, Brugh began looking for another project, in part to respond to continuing inquiries from potential users. Contiguous to the power center he found a 97-acre parcel that seemed well sized to serve as the next project. The parcel had been settled by the pioneering Flynn family as a farm and ranch. Brugh began negotiating a purchase agreement with the family matriarch, a strong-willed woman whom many people figured could not be persuaded to sell. She eventually agreed that the whole property should be zoned consistently and sold Brugh the rights to 40 acres, with Brugh footing most of the bill for the rezoning of the whole 97-acre tract.

The rezoning Brugh requested was to adopt a TND ordinance to guide the character of his mixed-use development. Brugh had been researching the TND approach for some time, prompted by conversations with an architect friend and his son's difficulties in finding affordable housing in the area. He came to understand the built-in value of TND neighborhood designs and wished to apply his new knowledge to a project that would include a mixed-use town center with an adjoining mix of residential development. He had offered in 1998 to pay for preparation of a TND ordinance by the Duany Plater-Zyberk firm, but the Missoula City-County Policy Planning Board declined, believing that a privately funded ordinance would give the appearance of an arranged zoning deal. Nevertheless, Brugh continued to discuss the virtues of TND with the Office of Planning and Grants.

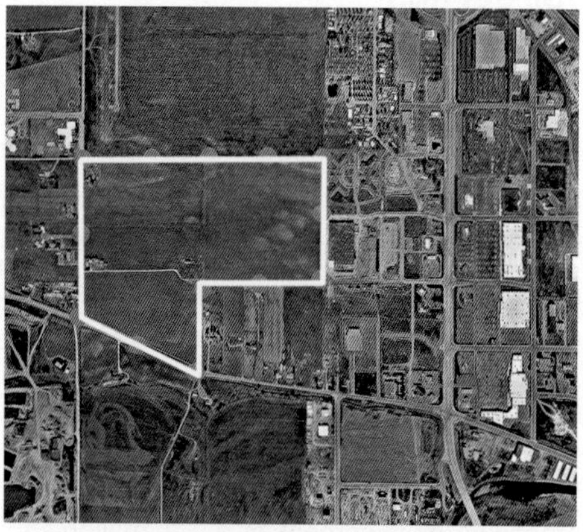

This aerial photo outlines the 97-acre tract of Hellgate Meadows, for which an overall plan was sketched during the charrette. More detailed design focused on the 40-acre initial development site, which adjoins a highway-oriented commercial development area, including "big-box" outlets.

When Brugh finally secured an option agreement from the Flynns in May 2000, Andrés Duany was traveling in China and unavailable for design consultation. Duany's firm recommended LCA Planners and Architects, LLC, of Portland, Oregon, as a suitable alternative. (The LCA firm was later acquired and merged with HDR, Inc. and Sargent to become HDR/LCA & Sargent Town Planning, now based in Ventura, California.)

Having spent time on the project for several years, Brugh had roughed out the potential components in his head. He knew he wanted a commercial and business center to accommodate the variety of potential clients who were asking for space—"a product of the demands of the marketplace," as he puts it. He also wanted to get his feet wet in the residential market, which he believed would be attracted by the easy walking distance to the stores and services in the retail center. He analyzed demographic trends in the area together with housing needs portrayed in the current Missoula Consolidated Plan to determine the range of housing types, including 44 units of affordable housing for seniors. Above all, he was fascinated by the opportunity to put a TND project together.

By this point, Brugh believed the time had come to air his thoughts about the project with the community and obtain broad input—and, hopefully, support for the project. He says that he entered into an outreach process to get his ideas on the table and to head off unwelcome surprises later on. He certainly won attention from community leaders, few of whom were familiar with the concept of traditional design in a modern setting. The process also served as an opportunity to work out some access issues with neighboring property owners and provided a way of engaging potential purchasers in the project. Brugh's attitude was and is: "Openness will give you the best results with the fewest surprises." He adds, "We weren't afraid of any wrong answers. We knew we had a good design idea and were satisfying many public needs."

THE PROCESS

Brugh brought in LCA Planners and Architects for an introductory public meeting on September 6, 2000. The meeting provided opportunities for attendees to get to know the site, explore the development possibilities, ask questions, and identify concerns. To stimulate responses, Bill Lennertz, an LCA principal at that time, floated ideas about the types of uses, varieties of building styles, and the potential size of the town center. He also described and showed slides of TND projects as examples of the design approach they intended to use. He kept the discussion free-flowing and informal, and productive in terms of positive feedback. He also described the nature of the proposed charrette to be held in a few weeks.

LCA had managed many charrettes, but this one demanded an unusually compressed time frame of four days, including one-on-one meetings with potential site users. On the positive side, the project was relatively small and the developer fairly certain about the kind of design approach he desired. LCA quickly focused on tackling design constraints and opportunities. The consultant team worked with Brugh and a local engineering firm familiar with the site and local codes to analyze the attributes of the site and sketch TND concepts for the entire 97-acre Flynn property. The team also checked ideas with a residential builder whom Brugh had brought into the deal. Ultimately, they prepared three different options for Brugh's 40 acres as well as the entire 97-acre site. Comments made at the public meeting helped to shape the designs.

The charrette took place on September 25 through September 28, 2000, at Hellgate Elementary School. Participants were invited by mail and word of mouth, and press releases were carried by the local newspaper. Although charrettes usually begin with a public meeting, this charrette began on Monday morning with the design team meeting with a series of potential buyers of parcels in the town center. Potential investors such as an accounting firm, a health club, assisted living residences, and churches were interested in sites, and the interviews allowed the consultants to ascertain their needs and respond to questions about the design concept.

That afternoon the public was invited to a general session to discuss design ideas for the project. Members of the Flynn family attended, as did community leaders and people associated with the university. The city's staff planners were fully involved, although only three of the 12 city council members participated. Two of the three county elected officials attended. Altogether, almost 50 people participated in the four-day process.

Their comments on Monday afternoon and the following days centered on traffic issues, such as connections with existing roads, and the living quality of the proposed development, such as the availability of parks. Overall, they were grateful for the opportunity to suggest ideas and watch the plan being developed. Brugh credits them with positive attitudes and says personality clashes were nonexistent.

On Tuesday morning, members of the consultant team met with city staff to discuss regulatory concerns about the TND approach and traffic issues as expressed the previous day (and anticipated by the developer). Meanwhile, work continued on refinements of the plans and sketches of details. They were the subject of a public "pin-up" session in the afternoon that gave participants an opportunity to see the latest iteration of the designs and discuss them directly with the designers. Design refinements and detailing continued through the evening.

On Wednesday morning, the team met with potential developers of affordable housing, office space, and daycare facilities, then used the remainder of the day and the next to work on drawings for the final presentation. The doors remained open for citizens to drop by at their convenience and submit additional comments. At 6:30 p.m. on Thursday, September 28, the consultant team presented the latest plan along with perspective renderings. Participants were asked to submit final comments for consideration in the revisions to take place after the charrette.

THE PLAN

The plan for the 40-acre site includes a mixed-use town center on the easternmost section, looking out across an elliptical green space to a mix of housing lining a grid of narrow streets. The town center grouped streetfront building clusters for a variety of retail shops and services and relatively high-density residential uses. Surface parking was to

The site plan for the initial 40-acre phase of development demonstrates the neotraditional character of planned development. The town center focuses on Flynn Green, and residential blocks fan out from the center along relatively narrow streets bordered by trees and sidewalks. Streets in the town center connect to the adjoining commercial development along the highway to allow residents to walk to retail stores.

be located in the rear of the buildings fronting on the green. The primary residential area spread west from the green to include 127 single-family houses on small lots (3,800 to 6,600 square feet) and 18 duplexes, townhomes, and rowhouses. All auto access to residential uses was from alleys. Residential street cross-sections incorporated sidewalks and planting strips on both sides of 20- to 26-foot roadways. The one-way loop around the green was limited to a 12-foot lane with two parking lanes and a 12-foot sidewalk. The new zoning regulations restrict architectural styles to those prevalent in Missoula from 1890 to 1935.

THE OUTCOME

During the months following the charrette, the consultant team revised the plans to reflect transportation, engineering, and other technical concerns and incorporate additional public comments. LCA developed a master plan for the entire site, a detailed plan for the easternmost 40 acres optioned by Brugh, and a set of zoning regulations and standards that could be adopted by the planning commission. The design package was completed in October 2000, and the TND ordinance to implement it was adopted by the city of Missoula on February 4, 2002.

As of January 2005, the following buildings have been completed and occupied in the town center:

- a 19,000-square-foot, two-story office building occupied by a regional accounting firm employing 40 people and an insurance company;
- a small veterinary clinic employing six people;
- a two-story office building occupied by a title insurance company;
- a 142-unit assisted living center;
- a 39-unit apartment building.

During the charrette, the consultants prepared renderings that illustrated the development concept. This drawing shows how Hellgate's town center surrounds Flynn Green, creating a true activity core for the whole development.

In addition, the local housing authority has purchased four lots for a 44-unit housing project for seniors, and a 30,500-square-foot health and fitness center is under construction.

The second phase of development includes 58 residential lots on which construction has been initiated or completed, including 32 single-family residences, four single-family residences that can accommodate persons with disabilities and/or live/work opportunities, five townhomes, five duplexes, and eight rowhouses. (Many of these homes near the town center were priced in the affordable range of $140,000 to $180,000 to enable purchase by first-time buyers; they have since escalated in value by about $40,000.) The third phase of 45 residential lots sold out in April 2005. All infrastructure improvements, including the green space, have been completed.

According to Brugh, the charrette helped cement public support for the innovative design, which enabled him to accommodate a variety of uses in an attractive setting. The home builders working on the site feature the special design on their Web sites and their marketing literature: "The first TND in the northern Rocky Mountain region." Brugh is preparing to launch another similarly designed project in the near future.

References:

Author telephone interviews with Bob Brugh, the developer, January 11 and 13, 2005; Bill Lennertz of the National Charrette Institute, Portland, Oregon, January 11, 2005; and Oliver Kuehne, LCA Town Planning & Architecture, LLC, January 31, 2005.

Bob Brugh review of draft case study.

LCA Web site: www.lcaarchitects.com, Hellgate Meadows project summary.

Hellgate Web site: www.hellgatemeadows.com.

Missoula Web site: www.missoula.montana.com.

Case Study

North St. Lucie County, Florida, Comprehensive Plan Charrette

The county sponsored a seven-day charrette with small-group meetings to reach consensus on a master plan to guide future development in a rapidly growing rural area. Many charrette participants later turned out to support the plan.

A consultant team headed by the staff of the Treasure Coast Regional Planning Council worked with officials and citizens of St. Lucie County, Florida, to prepare a "citizens master plan" for the northern section of the county. This was a publicly sponsored effort to agree on a planning concept that would guide more detailed planning, as well as on an implementation program for development that was already spreading westward from the coastal area. Centered around a seven-day charrette, followed by more detailed studies and plans, it represents a popular approach to establishing broad consensus about the character of future growth.

THE SETTING

St. Lucie County is one of the string of counties along the southeast coast of Florida affected by growth pushing north from the Miami/Fort Lauderdale region. The county's population has grown by 42 percent in just ten years, from 150,171 in 1990 to 213,500 in 2000. In ten more years an additional 50,000 or so residents are expected. The wave of development is replacing rural open space with new development and overrunning small communities. One of the county's attractions is a low cost of living, exemplified in housing prices that average $80,000 for a three-bedroom, two-bath home and $125,000 for an oceanfront condominium. Economically, St. Lucie County depends mostly on service employment; the job base is centered on school, medical, and retail activities.

North St. Lucie County is defined as the area between the intracoastal waterway on the east, past the I-95 highway on the west, and from the C25 canal on the south to the northern county boundary. Development in this 28-square-mile agricultural area was raising troubling issues. Urban development in North St. Lucie County occurs in a band along the Old Dixie Highway at the coastline, and in a number of large-scale developments just inland from the coast. Some of these developments are gated golf-course communities; others are platted for single-family homes at densities of up to five units per acre. Elsewhere in the area, the predominant use is agriculture, primarily citrus groves. Dotted among the groves are houses, usually on five or more acres of land, whose owners often are involved in some form of rural activity, such as raising garden crops or keeping horses. Most of the area is zoned for one-acre lots.

In recent years, however, developers have stepped up the pressure for westward expansion of the county's urban service line to allow higher density development. Ownership of land between the urban service boundary and the I-95 highway began changing hands as developers moved to option potential development sites. Residents of the rural area grew increasingly alarmed at what they viewed as a wave of premature urban development, one that would threaten their way of life and the agricultural economy of the northwestern part of the county.

The county commissioners responded by employing the Treasure Coast Regional Planning Council to conduct a charrette-centered process to formulate a new master plan for the northern section of the county. In Florida's growth management system, the planning council is one of many blanketing the state. It is responsible for regional planning for the area of Palm Beach, Martin, St. Lucie, and Indian River counties. Over the years, it has won a reputation for design-based planning often focused on small towns, downtowns, and neighborhoods, but also for tackling large-scale planning issues such as those arising in St. Lucie County. Its work is well known by county officials. One commissioner is a member of the council's board, and all the commissioners had worked with council staff on various planning projects in the past.

It was understood that the "citizens' plan" would require additional effort to be translated into an implementation program.

The planning council's four-person design team headed up the process, assisted by representatives of four design and planning firms and eight urban designers who brought special talents. The council took as its assignment the creation of a master plan that would represent the citizens' vision for the future of North St. Lucie County. The plan would be expressed in drawings and sketches to illustrate the most appropriate forms of development and open space conservation. It was understood that the "citizens' plan" would require additional effort to be translated into an implementation program.

THE PROCESS

The professional staff of the planning council has organized and managed many types of workshops, but likes to focus on charrettes as a productive form of community engagement. Some are held over a five-day period, others up to nine days. In this case, after evaluating the development issues to be considered, the staff recommended a seven-day charrette that would allow plenty of time for citizen input in evaluating all the issues. The design team held six organizational meetings with a steering committee formed of county staff and community leaders representing various parts of the North St. Lucie area. Then in the week before the charrette, the team conducted a series of one-on-one interviews with stakeholder interests—major property owners, public officials, developers, land use attorneys—to sound out issues and concerns likely to arise during charrette discussions.

Meanwhile, potential participants were being informed about the charrette. Residents were aware of the upcoming event because the county commissioners' work in setting up the process had been widely reported. The usual flyers and media announcements publicized the starting date and expected schedule. Members of the steering committee, which included representatives of many neighborhoods and towns, were also enjoined to spread the word among their neighbors. The door-to-door nature of this process succeeded in attracting a large number of participants, many of whom stayed involved throughout the week-long exercise.

Over 350 participants showed up for the first event held on Saturday, February 7, 2004—according to project manager Marcela Camblor, more than the planning council had ever attracted to a charrette. The first hour or so was spent bringing the participants up to speed on the study area definition and the issues and concerns that had surfaced during the planning council's interviews. Examples of planning and design elsewhere were described to illustrate the opportunities available to North St. Lucie. The staff then articulated some basic principles as a starting point for the formulation of the master plan, subject, of course, to further discussion and agreement by participants:

1. Retain large areas of the countryside in rural, open, and undeveloped condition;
2. Develop a central backbone system for water management in contrast to project-by-project, individual solutions;
3. Provide an interconnected system of greenways, parks, and open spaces;
4. Incorporate an interconnected network of streets in a predictable manner;
5. Locate public, institutional, retail, and service uses in proximity to and at an appropriate scale for new settlements;

6. Reorganize land use entitlements to allow for transfer of development rights to preserve the natural environment;

7. Accommodate the next 50 years of anticipated growth in terms that meet community interests;

8. Create a predictable development pattern for the benefit of investors and citizens alike;

9. Maintain the urban service boundary in its present location.

Participants in the charrette in North St. Lucie County were able to trade ideas on development issues in the "real space" shown on area maps.

Instead of continuing strip commercial development along major roads, the new plan proposes to cluster commercial and service buildings within a grid of pedestrian-friendly streets, as illustrated by this sketch of one such center.

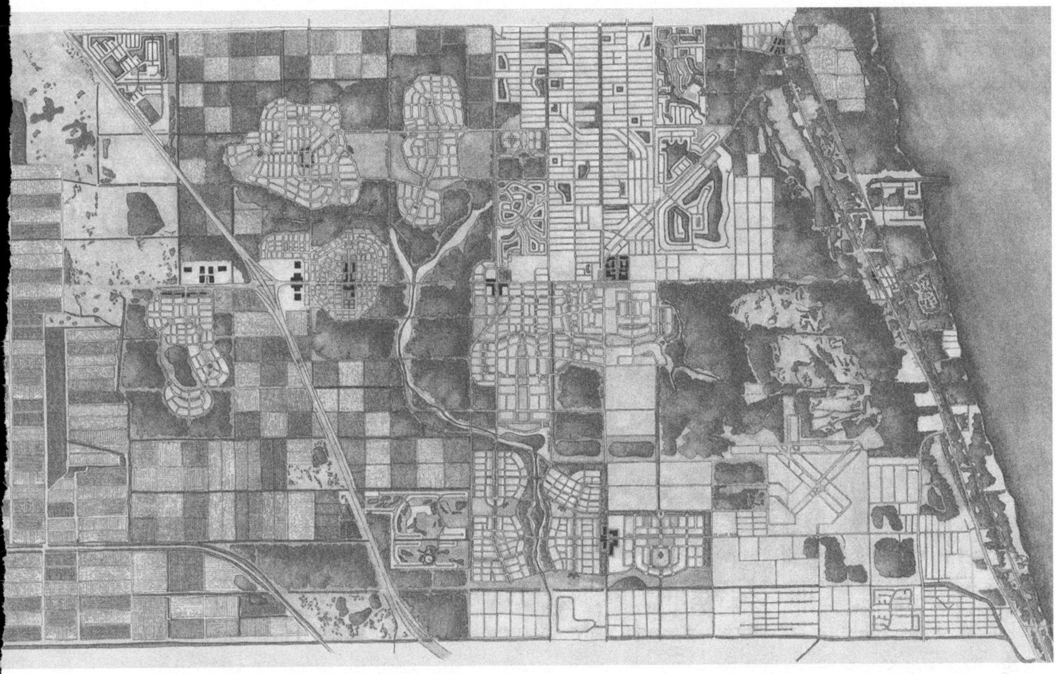

The "Citizens' Master Plan" for North St. Lucie County contains development within infill neighborhoods and compact hamlets and villages, thus allowing conservation of important natural features such as the "backbone" system for water management, a new county park, and preserved countryside.

The participants then were grouped around tables—normally eight to ten per table but because of the large turnout about 20 per table. Aided by a design facilitator, they were asked to draw plans that represented how the North St. Lucie area should grow. After about three hours, reporters from each table described their ideas, which became inputs for the design work that followed. The drawings were kept for constant reference by the consultant team.

For the remainder of the week, the staff labored over drawing plans and sketches depicting various land use concepts, detailed illustrations of development options, and examples of streetscapes, town centers, and the like. They produced a computer-simulated series of maps showing existing development and the progression of development over time according to the current plan, ending in buildout in about 2025 with the entire area developed. Other drawings depicted how agricultural and natural areas could be preserved to provide for water management and a system of greenways and parks, while still allowing significant development clustered in a few areas. Photographs of streets functioning as desirable public spaces and of various types of public buildings providing an attractive civic presence illustrated opportunities for creating livable neighborhoods. Sketches of hamlets, villages, and towns showed how grouping urban uses within the open space network could accommodate development without losing the rural sense of place. Computer-generated animation of these sketches revealed how these places would look as viewed by a driver along a main street or from a plane. This helped participants who had problems envisioning the three-dimensional qualities of two-dimensional drawings.

The staff did not labor in isolation. The studio remained open for charrette participants to wander in and review and comment on the latest ideas. Some 50 to 60 citizens visited the studio every day. At times, the designers would sit with small groups to explain design ideas and test responses. Late-afternoon pin-up sessions allowed citizens to drop in after work for a quick scan of the latest drawings. Through it all, the design team looked to participants for reactions and direction. Later in the week, the design team met twice with the steering committee to review progress and present an early draft of a set of recommendations.

At one point, the consultant team scheduled a special meeting with county officials and staff to avert a potential confrontation over a policy issue. The consultants and charrette participants had worked out a concept for using transferable development rights as an incentive for clustered development in otherwise rural areas. However, the consultants found that the county staff's views on the concept differed from theirs. The meeting that brought together the key decision makers, including charrette participants, helped to resolve the issue.

The Treasure Coast Regional organization contracted for the work for a fee of $85,000. Executive Director Michael J. Busha says that the staff contributed at least $60,000 in additional time on the job. He compared those costs to the budget probably required for employing a private consultant team for such a project, which he estimated at up to $250,000.

THE OUTCOME

Committee members' comments were reflected in the final presentation, which was made on Friday, February 13. It was successful enough that many of the charrette participants turned out to support the plan at the more formal presentation to the county commissioners a month later.

At the end of this session, the county commissioners instructed staff to initiate a follow-up $1 million work program, including drafting of comprehensive plan amendments, an analysis of fiscal impact and financing needs, and implementation of land use regulations and programs. The Treasure Coast RPC is managing the work program. The steering committee is to maintain involvement in the process. The target date for accomplishing this implementation program is the end of fiscal year 2005.

References:

Author telephone interviews with Marcela Camblor, director of the TCRPC Design Studio, January 17 and February 2, 2005.

North St. Lucie County Charrette. Prepared by the Treasure Coast Regional Planning Council for St. Lucie County, February 2004.

Case Study Pleasant Hill BART Station, California

After years caught in a bitter standstill, a developer and two public agencies collaborated with a citizens' advisory group to determine a development plan for the BART station area that received unanimous approval from the County Board of Supervisors.

Long-term controversies over transit-oriented development around the Bay Area Rapid Transit (BART) station in the San Francisco Bay Area community of Pleasant Hill were settled through a charrette process commissioned by a triumvirate of Contra Costa County, the BART system, and the developer already selected to carry out the development. This collaborative venture finally brought agreement on a specific plan for development that met the objectives of all three principals as well as local participants.

THE SETTING

According to Michael Bernick and Robert Cervero's *Transit Villages in the 21st Century*, the Pleasant Hill BART Station area planning process has "advanced the cause of transit village development more than any other station on the [BART] system." Nevertheless, the road to that achievement has been long and conflictive. For almost 20 years, development around the station proceeded steadily but never quite jelled to create an attractive, walkable center. Efforts beginning in 1995 to adopt a plan for the area immediately around the station stalled in the face of strong opposition to various proposals. Then in 2001, a week-long charrette process broke the logjam and led to a consensus plan that is being implemented today.

Efforts to spur transit-focused development at the suburban, sparsely developed Pleasant Hill station area were launched in 1977 when the county's Board of Supervisors adopted a general plan amendment for transit-oriented development. By 1981, however, acknowledging that little development had taken place around the station in the ten years since it opened, a committee of representatives of Contra Costa County, the cities of Walnut Creek and Pleasant Hill, and BART commissioned the preparation of a specific plan for the 140-acre area within a quarter mile of the station.

The plan for what is now called Contra Costa Centre proposed a concentration of high-intensity office uses within 700 feet of the station, multifamily housing further out, and then single-family housing beyond that, all with retail uses and public open spaces mingled with other uses. Development gradually occurred around the station according to the plan, assisted by property assemblage and infrastructure improvements provided by the Contra Costa County Redevelopment Agency and the formation of the Contra Costa Centre Association, a marketing/management group. By the end of 1994, development within a quarter mile of the station amounted to over 1,600 residential units, mostly in high-rise buildings, 1.5 million square feet of office space, and a 249-room hotel. Surveys indicated that 10 percent of local employees used BART and 60 percent of residents said that access to BART was a major factor in moving there.

OBSTACLES ENCOUNTERED

In 1996, Bernick and Cervero determined that over half the land in the station area remained undeveloped, including three large parcels near the station. Completed buildings were unconnected to each other and to the station, and retail and public open space was conspicuous by its absence. Two large parking lots adjacent to the BART station and two major streets interrupted pedestrian flows. Several problems stood in the way of completing development. Nearby neighborhood organizations, including a swim club in the path of development, actively opposed dense development around the station. The cities of Walnut Creek and Pleasant Hill wanted to lure development to their downtown areas rather than promote it around the station. In addition, the 1989 Loma Prieta earthquake and the real estate recession of the late 1980s and early 1990s caused postponement of several planned projects. By the mid-1990s, development around the station had ground to a halt.

In early 1995, BART attempted to jump-start additional development by issuing a request for proposals (RFP) for development of 11.4 acres of parking lots in the 18.8-acre BART

This view of the station area at Pleasant Hill shows the amount of space taken up by surface parking—a land bank for the future development that was planned during the week-long charrette.

station property. A development team headed by Millennium Partners won approval for a massive entertainment complex that would capitalize on opportunities for shared parking and establish the Pleasant Hill station area as an important destination. About the same time, the redevelopment agency issued an RFP for residential development for another site, and a third project to construct 200 residential units was proposed.

The proposed entertainment center ran into a buzzsaw of opposition. Major issues included:

- Objections of three cities around the site to a project that would compete with their downtown areas;
- Competition among the cities about which would annex the area;
- Rejection by the Commuters Alliance, representing park-and-ride transit users, of the concept of turning 581 temporary parking spaces along the BART rail right-of-way into green space;
- Opposition by many members of a swim club to its property being acquired by the county to provide replacement parking.

After two years of controversy, the developer withdrew the proposal, although Millennium Partners remained committed to eventual development of the property.

BACK TO THE DRAWING BOARD

In 1997, the county redevelopment agency began a two-year process of amending the specific plan for the station area, focused on reaching agreement on the future development of the parking lot site. The amended plan cut densities of development, including decreases of about one-third of the allowable development on the BART property. The plan also called for community participation in planning for site development, but after one sparsely attended meeting the procedure stopped. Eventually, Donna Gerber, a county supervisor, picked up the ball. She brought in Peter Katz from the Congress for New Urbanism for a lecture to interested citizens about the principles of the new urbanism. She then formed a committee including one of the principal opponents of the previous plan, the Walnut District Improvement Association, to consider selection of a consultant familiar with the new urbanism to help agree on a detailed development plan for the 18-acre BART site. In 2000, the Contra Costa County Redevelopment Agency employed Lennertz, Coyle & Associates, subsequently reorganized as LCA Planners and Architects, from Portland, Oregon, to conduct a charrette to achieve that goal. (Bill Lennertz now heads up the Charrette Institute in Portland, Oregon, and LCA Planners and Architects is now part of HDR/LCA and Sargent Town Planning of Ventura, California.)

THE PROCESS

The lead consultant group for the Pleasant Hill charrette, LCA Planners and Architects, had organized dozens of charrettes and similar exercises. It led a consultant team that included architects, landscape architects, engineers, economists, and transportation and transit engineers. The firm reported to a triumvirate of organizations directly responsible for the project: BART, the county redevelopment agency, and Millennium Partners, the designated development firm. From time to time, that group was augmented by representatives of other agencies and organizations for ratification of major decisions.

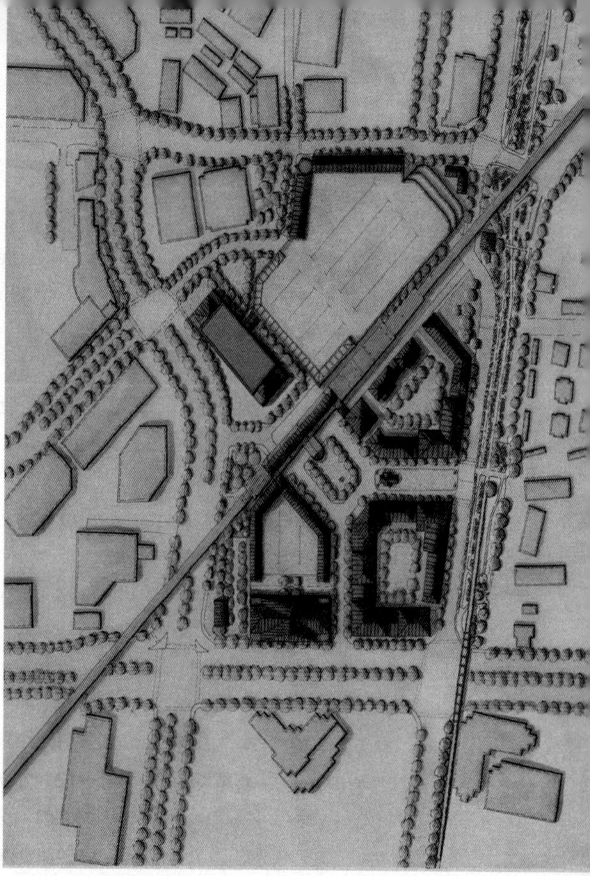

The plan for Pleasant Hill shows the office building and parking structure across the tracks from the station, and the residential blocks (with some retail frontage) completing the development, all focused around pedestrian-friendly areas leading to the station.

Beginning in the fall of 2000, the team undertook five major tasks in preparation for the charrette:

- Getting to know the physical and economic context by analyzing site conditions and development opportunities;
- Interviewing individuals and representatives of jurisdictions and organizations to identify key leaders and important issues emanating from past planning processes and current conditions;
- Developing a couple of design concepts to spark discussions at the charrette;
- Working out the types and sequence of activities (subject to continuous review and adaptation) and determining assignments for leading and guiding the discussions;
- Establishing a variety of communications mechanisms for publicizing the purposes and schedule for the charrette.

In addition to the conflictive history of planning for the area, the site offered plenty of problems to overcome: heavily trafficked roads on three sides, limited street connections into surrounding neighborhoods, a seven-story parking garage in the middle of the site, the BART station and tracks cutting through the site, and high groundwater levels that limited underground parking. However, the BART station and adjoining highways provided good regional access and an existing park, a grove of oak trees, and a planned trail connection supplied amenities.

The consultant team held pre-charrette meetings with key stakeholders and community organizations, individual meetings with neighborhood leaders in their homes, a large public meeting to explain the planning process being initiated, and a "movers and shakers" reception to raise awareness among business and political leaders about the goals of the process. According to Bill Lennertz, Supervisor Gerber and her staff helped to identify key leaders; a community liaison consultant provided names and e-mail addresses for many people potentially interested in the plan, including many who had not attended previous planning meetings. The consultants also organized a bus tour before the charrette.

The big issues continued to be traffic and density, although the latter concern was muted by the revised specific plan that reduced allowable high-rise development. But concerns continued about replacing BART's surface parking within the site, keeping the retail presence low, and constructing the Iron Horse Trail that had been promised for years. The goal of the outreach efforts was to involve as many people as possible, including individuals and organizations that had not participated in past events.

The team established a temporary studio in the Embassy Suites Hotel from February 22 through February 27, 2001, and announced that it would be open from 8:30 a.m. to 9:30 p.m. each of those days. Illustrated postcards were mailed to residents and businesses in the area to publicize the dates, times, and purposes of the events. Other notices were posted in the station and made available to train passengers. The E-mail list was constantly used to remind potential participants about upcoming events. A project Web site was created and a local cable television station broadcast announcements.

The charrette was planned to allow at least three cycles of design proposals followed by intense evaluations by participants. LCA designed the process to allow ideas to bubble up, circulate within groups, receive technical analysis and input, and then be packaged with others in revised designs. On a day-to-day basis, the plan evolved as follows:

- **Day 1:** At a public review session attended by over 200 people, the design team presented two design concepts showing alternative street patterns and building sites, and led whole-group and small-group discussions to identify the pros and cons of the alternatives;

- **Day 2:** While the public was free to study informational displays and discuss concerns one-on-one with team members, the consultant team prepared refinements to the plans based on the feedback from Day 1;

- **Day 3:** At another public session the revised designs, indicating major differences in sites for important components, were presented and evaluated by participants in small-group discussions; one design that gained favor was enhanced by participant suggestions;

- **Day 4:** The design team reviewed the favored plan to identify and resolve any technical problems and to make detailed studies of market and financial feasibility;

Day 5: About 50 people participated in a transportation focus group to discuss transportation impacts of the emerging design;

Day 6: Based on strong interest in increasing residential development, the design team presented a design that maximized the amount of housing and green space to an evening meeting attended by nearly 200 people.

Lennertz says the process worked, but tensions were high at times. At the opening meeting, he was in the midst of presenting two sketch designs intended to break the ice and start discussion when audience members objected. They were not attending to hear about the consultant's plan, they said, but to get their concerns and ideas on the table. The meeting was reformatted on the spot to allow residents to speak up. Neighborhood residents had put their own strategy together. It called for maximizing residential development to lower traffic and alleviate the visual effects of new large office buildings.

Anxieties about traffic continued to roil charrette discussions until the consultants organized a small-group meeting to focus on the problem. The transportation consultant calmed things down with a detailed explanation of potential reductions in traffic generation and increases in travel capacity, including better use of transit and construction of the proposed trail that neighborhood residents had desired for years. The consultants also won favor by taking time during the charrette to retest traffic counts on the site, which some residents believed had increased markedly since the counts taken several years earlier. (They hadn't.)

Another significant issue was replacing the parking lot that would be used for new development. The county had pinned hopes on acquiring the property used by the swim club. But older members who were pleased to sell the property were opposed by newer, younger members who wished to keep the club operating. Finally, it was agreed that the parking would be consolidated in a large parking structure next to the station. Due to the considerably higher costs stemming from that decision, further discussion determined that the replacement parking would be funded through a complicated county/BART deal rather than by the developer.

This drawing details the view toward the station and residential blocks, illustrating the green spaces that will welcome commuters and other pedestrians.

This drawing illustrated the BART station area's potential to welcome vistors—and to become a future landmark in Pleasant Hill.

THE PLAN

To residents' satisfaction, the new plan boosted residential development—for a total of 560 units—and capped office development at one high-rise building. (Recent market changes supported residential development over near-term office development.) Meanwhile, the amount of retail space became a non-issue as the developer's market analysis determined limited appeal for such uses. Charrette participants even obtained BART's promise to sell land—against its longstanding policy—to enable building of 110 for-sale townhomes and live/work units.

The final plan is a strong place-making statement for Pleasant Hill. It incorporates a formal civic space at Station Square surrounded by a mix of commercial and civic uses, an elegant residential street connecting Station Square with the Iron Horse Trail, a 12-story office building visually linking the station to existing office buildings, retention of the oak grove as a park, and accommodation of all parking needs subject to further feasibility studies.

The project plan for the Pleasant Hill station area was drawn on an aerial photo to illustrate the plan's three-dimensional qualities.

THE OUTCOME

The charrette enabled participants with heretofore divisive views to understand the benefits of a unified plan. In 2002, the Contra Costa County Board of Supervisors voted unanimously to adopt the plan and the regulatory documents drawn up by the consultants to implement it. The first step in development is construction of the new BART parking garage, which will free up land for the remaining development.

This experience demonstrates how an informed consultant team can help overcome differences in goals and perceptions by establishing a neutral venue that allows a consideration of tradeoffs among divergent views. With skilled assistance, community representatives can learn from the process to enrich project planning and design that enable a workable balance between community and developer goals.

References:

Bernick, Michael and Robert Cervero. *Transit Villages in the 21st Century.* New York: McGraw-Hill, 1997.

Still, Katherine Gray, G.B. Arrington, and Topaz Faulkner. "Pleasant Hill, Contra Costa County, California." (Draft case study prepared for ULI, July 2001).

LCA Town Planning & Architecture, LLC Web site: www.lcaarchitects.com/casestudies, "LCA Charrette Case Study," 2004.

"Pleasant Hill BART Station Area Community Plan, Summary Report," October 2001. Available at www.ccreach.org.

Author interviews with Jim Kennedy, Contra Costa County Community Development Department, April 19, 2002, and December 20, 2004.

Author interviews with Bill Lennertz, National Charrette Institute, Portland, Oregon, December 10 and 20, 2004.

Case Study
Rolling Mill Hill, Nashville, Tennessee

Through a city-county–sponsored process centered on a series of three workshops, land use and design policies were established for development, which quickly will be creating new opportunities for developers selected after proposals are reviewed by the redevelopment agency.

Nashville's city-county development and housing agency sponsored a community outreach process to formulate a redevelopment plan for a city-owned area next to downtown. The plan, mostly for residential uses, had to take into account the reuse of historic structures and an untested market for in-town housing. Through a process centered on three workshops, a broadly representative committee reached agreement on a plan and phased development program. After requesting developer proposals, the agency will select one of a short list of six offers for the first phase of development.

THE SETTING

Rolling Mill Hill is a 34-acre redevelopment area next to downtown Nashville, acquired over a number of years by the Metropolitan Development and Housing Agency. The site is on a bluff overlooking the Cumberland River and adjoins Gateway Boulevard, one of the primary access routes to downtown Nashville. Much of the site was a wasteland of parking lots and disused buildings. Residential uses had gradually declined, a complex of trolley barns was serving temporary uses, and the historic former General Hospital buildings had been vacant for years. With the goal of creating a mixed-use model of smart growth infill development, the agency had advertised for developer interest in redevelopment of the property. Attempts to work out rebuilding strategies with two firms were found financially infeasible, chiefly due to the high infrastructure costs of preparing the site for development.

With this background, the agency determined to launch its own redevelopment project. It sought to create a mix of marketable uses with a focus on in-town housing, and a plan that would take advantage of the site's proximity to the riverfront and downtown. It also hoped that successful redevelopment of the property could spark future improvement efforts in the adjoining neighborhood.

Nashville has long employed community outreach processes to assist in formulating neighborhood and downtown improvement plans. A recently completed, lengthy effort to

Some of the historic and rather grand old hospital buildings, here viewed from the I-24 bridge over the river, will be preserved as the centerpiece of a new residential neighborhood near downtown.

update its comprehensive plan for the metropolitan area drew the involvement of many citizens and proved highly useful in educating the public about urban design issues. Design workshops and charrettes are familiar discussion formats for many Nashville community leaders. When the agency announced the launching of a community engagement program for Rolling Mill Hill, it could count on the involvement of an educated public accustomed to evaluating development opportunities and framing attractive and feasible redevelopment plans.

To head up the consultant team for the engagement process, the Authority employed RTKL Associates, Inc., of Washington, D.C., an architecture and design firm that had prepared an earlier plan for the area for one of the firms interested in redeveloping the site. To the team were added a local architectural firm and specialists in economic market studies, architecture, landscape architecture, land planning, and traffic engineering. The local architectural firm was especially knowledgeable about community movers and shakers who could provide leadership in the planning process; the firm also was familiar with the local development codes and key members of public agencies. Another local person signed on to act as the meeting organizer and facilitator.

The process was focused around a series of three workshops, preceded by several weeks of market and design analyses and followed by intensive labor to complete a final plan and recommendations for an implementation program. From the beginning, expectations regarding the form and content of future development were relatively firm. Redevelopment was understood to be a given, not an issue, especially since the agency owned all the land. Planning objectives for redevelopment were defined by the agency and design team as follows:

- Create a lively urban neighborhood with a sense of place to support community identity and a high-quality public realm;
- Reinforce vehicular and pedestrian connections to the riverfront and the adjacent Rutledge Hill neighborhood;

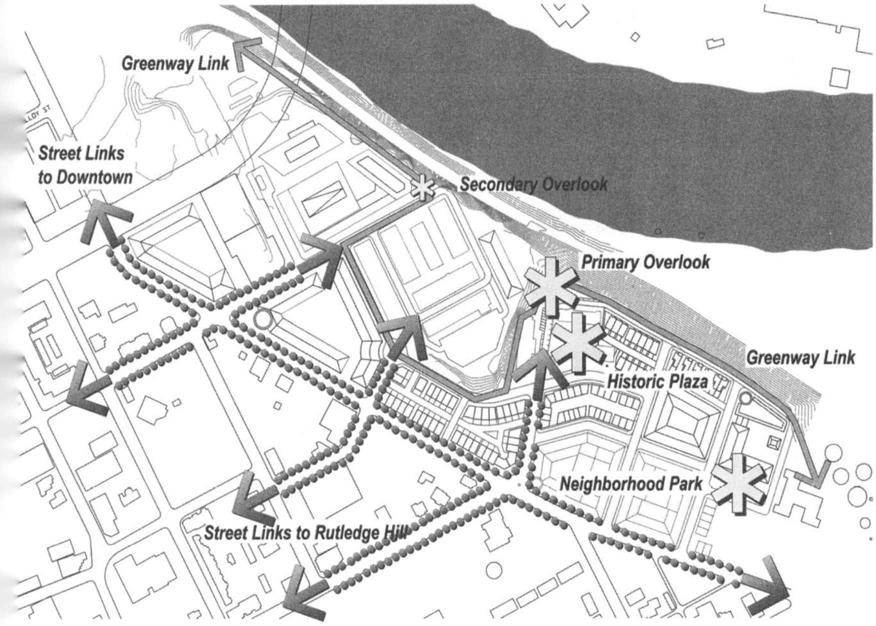

The consultant's design analysis for Rolling Mill Hill identified key open space opportunities as an organizing context for future development.

- Develop most of the site for a range of urban housing types and for a mix of incomes;
- Adapt historic structures for compatible uses as feasible.

The agency and design team also identified some concerns to be resolved, including the potential reuse of the trolley barns, the extent of future retail development in this area near downtown, the depth of market attraction for new in-town housing, and the incorporation of other uses such as offices and hotels.

The consultant team spent about six weeks assessing market opportunities and identifying design constraints and assets on and near the site. The team noted the fine views from the site across the river and to downtown, the lack of neighborhood identity within the site and its surrounding area, and the untested market but potential pent-up demand for higher-density urban living opportunities in the area. Team members also met with staff of metro agencies (Nashville is a consolidated city and county) to determine their concerns and ongoing plans.

ENGAGING THE COMMUNITY

Word about the community outreach effort was spread through a number of media routes: the agency Web site and links on related Web sites, flyers posted in the neighborhoods, an advertisement in the community newspaper, and especially by word of mouth among community and neighborhood leaders. A broad range of participants responded, including a few of the residents still living in the area, local business representatives, members of community groups, some public officials, and several planners, architects, and developers interested in the area's future development.

The first workshop on May 21, 2003 attracted about 70 participants. The consultant team members introduced themselves and described the process they would undertake. Then they presented the features of in-town, new urbanist neighborhood design that would guide their planning for future development, including the smaller lots, narrower

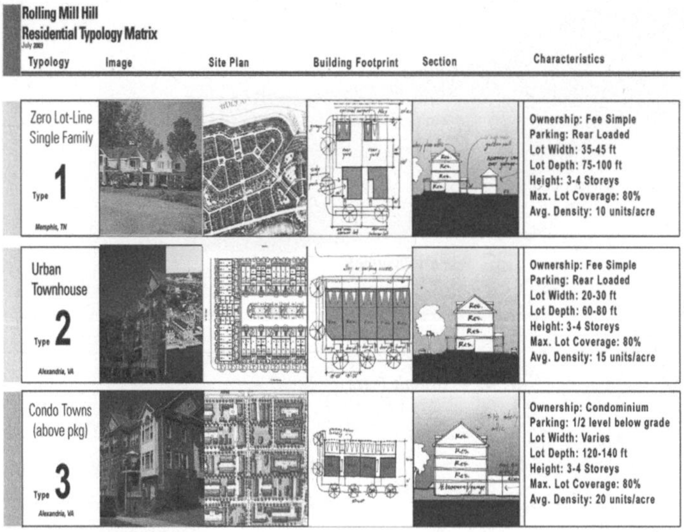

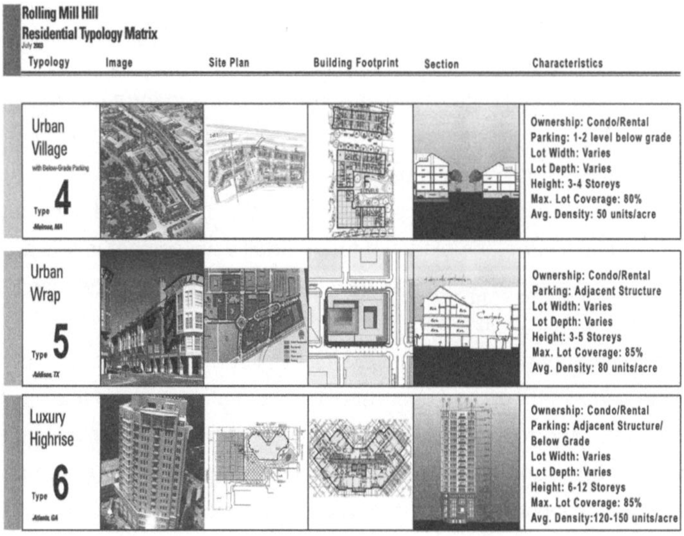

For consideration by the advisory group, the design team described an array of potential types of residential buildings suitable for the Rolling Mill Hill location.

streets, civic spaces, and other aspects of higher-density living environments. As part of the presentation they described a typology of urban housing designs, demonstrating how well-designed in-town housing could appeal to people accustomed to suburban living. They emphasized that the untested housing market for this area presented a challenge to create a pleasing living environment that would attract suburbanites to this location.

Participants were then grouped ten to a table, each with a design facilitator to guide discussion. The team leader, Bill Caldwell of RTKL, comments that the table facilitators were hardly needed as people eagerly went to work to list key features and concerns about the development of the area. Among their comments about future uses and design aspects:

- There should be a focus on residential uses with a mix of households (renter and owner) and incomes;
- Some retail shops and services should be well located to serve the neighborhood; small offices and a hotel also would be compatible with other uses;

- An elementary school would be appropriate if demand warranted it and other community amenities and services would be important to establish a pleasant living environment;
- Public access to the riverfront was an important asset to preserve open views across the river and take advantage of the character of the bluff;
- Reuse of historic buildings, especially some of the hospital buildings, would help to re-create neighborhood identity, although the one-story trolley barns presented difficulties for adaptive use;
- The scale and character of new development should be in line with the existing neighborhood, although some mid-rise and high-rise buildings would be acceptable if they did not block views; and
- People desired a walkable community.

These established some basic concepts for the design team to incorporate in preliminary plans and drawings. Two sketch plans were prepared for evaluation at the next meeting, on June 11. One plan assumed somewhat higher density development than the other; building forms and open spaces were differentiated but the mix of uses was similar. The 70 or so participants were divided into three groups to evaluate the alternative plans. Generally, they liked the mix of uses, although the extent and location of retail uses remained uncertain. They were interested in creating an open space network connecting to a riverfront greenway; street and walking patterns received considerable attention. Most participants preferred that high-rise buildings be located at the edge rather than the center of the area. Reuse of the trolley barns remained a goal but specific proposals were uncertain, given the one-story, lackluster design of the buildings.

THE PLAN

By this point in the process, the consultant team believed it had a sufficient understanding of community concerns and interests to proceed with completing the plan. (The team had been germinating many elements of the plan during the earlier stages of the process.) The plan actually was to consist of a series of maps, drawings, and related text, all packaged as development guidelines and including:

- An illustrative plan showing how the new development might appear when fully implemented and indicating major elements, relationships to Rutledge Hill, and the qualities of public spaces;
- A land use plan identifying types of residential uses (e.g., zero lot line, urban townhouse) recommended for various areas and the locations of community, office, and retail uses;
- A parcel plan and phasing strategy;
- A framework plan showing the street network supplemented by drawings of street sections indicating pavements, sidewalks, street trees, and yard spaces;

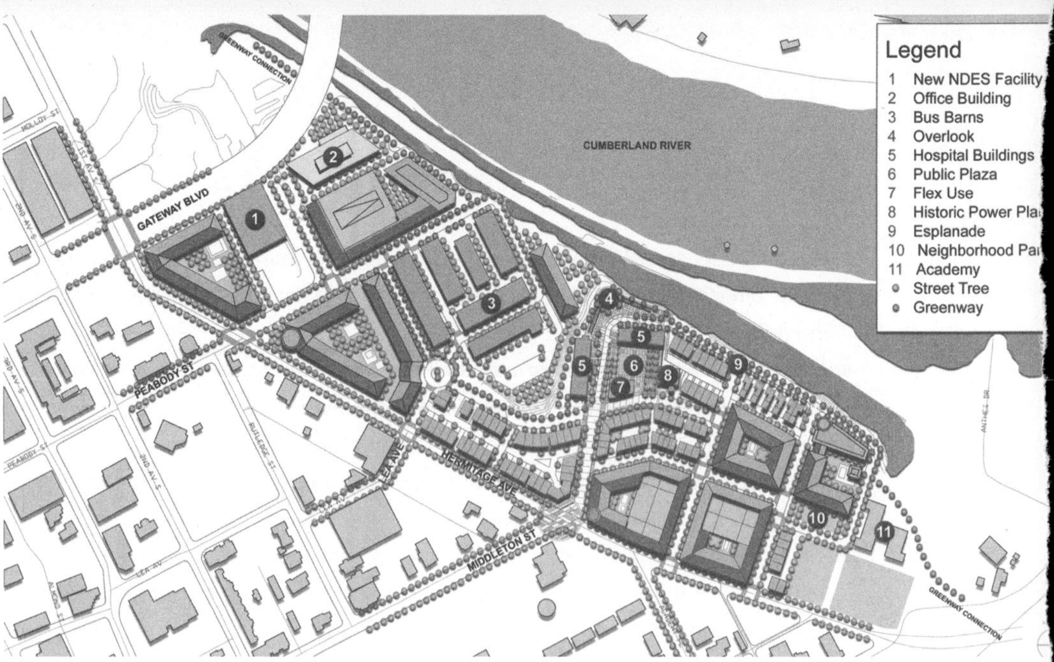

After considering several sketch plans of potential development, this plan was selected by the advisory group as representing the best design relationships of historic and new buildings and the variety of desired uses.

- An open space plan indicating open space connections to adjoining areas and the key qualities of public open spaces;
- Streetscape standards and development guidelines for builders, indicating urban design objectives, scale and massing of buildings, exterior building appearance, and signage standards; and
- A financial analysis of the proposed plan that determined the capability of the proposed development for generating funding for required infrastructure improvements; the strategy counted on careful phasing of development to leverage value increases during early development.

The completed plan rested on the outcome of several decisions evolved during the community engagement process. One was a street grid similar in scale to that of the adjacent Rutledge Hill neighborhood. The greenway along the river bluff, with a public overlook, was extended as a pedestrian pathway from downtown through the project and hopefully farther east. A public plaza defined by surrounding buildings will serve as the heart of the new neighborhood. A few retail uses were located to serve the neighborhood. Three of the historic hospital buildings will be restored; one (the former power house and chimney) will be used as a community center. Attempts will continue to find suitable uses for the trolley barns.

The draft framework plan and development guidelines were presented at the third community meeting on August 6, about seven weeks after the previous meeting. Fewer people—about 50—attended this session, presumably because process participants had had their input and were satisfied with the outcome. One question was the final gross density of the proposed development, which is about 33 dwelling units per acre. Another question concerned the role of the agency in development of the site. The agency indicated that it would play the role of master developer and either sell parcels or become an equity partner in land deals, depending on the circumstances at the time. In any case, the agency intended to find committed developers to work with over several years.

A final question concerned phasing and timing of development. The basic strategy is to leverage the prime assets of the site—the views and historic sense of place—to jump-

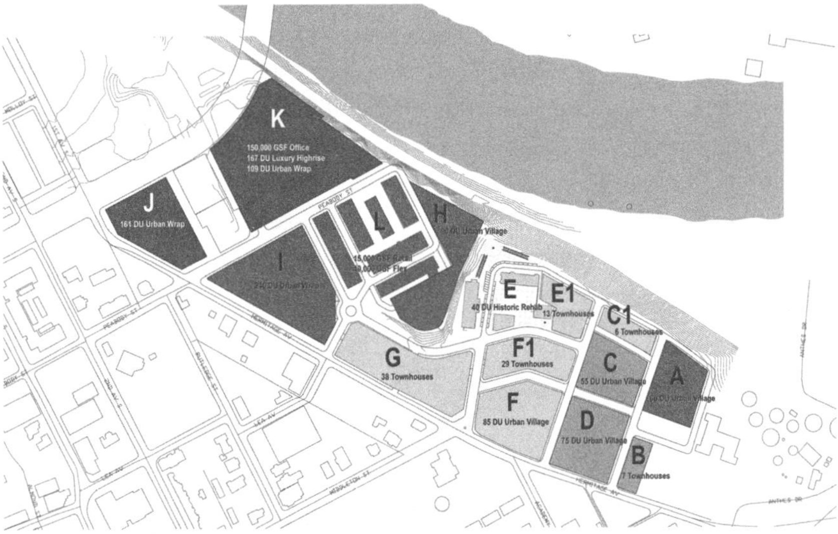

The final phasing plan for Rolling Mill Hill shows the variety of uses planned for the area and the expected sequence of requests for development by the redevelopment agency.

start the development process. The agency hopes that higher prices generated in the first phase will enable higher-density development in later phases.

RTKL's consulting team for the Rolling Mill Hill project required a budget of about $235,000 for work with local officials and neighborhood residents over a period of six months or so. The work product, including recommendations for buildings sites, uses, and phasing made it possible for the redevelopment agency to immediately request developer proposals for construction on key sites.

THE OUTCOME

Throughout the summer of 2004, the agency worked with local consultants to develop plans for new infrastructure improvements on Rolling Mill Hill, including new streets, underground wiring, sewer and stormwater systems, site grading, greenways, and streetscapes. The development of these facilities, in addition to demolition of nonhistoric structures, will enable the agency to offer "pad-ready" sites for developers.

On August 30, 2004, the agency issued a request for qualifications (RFQ) from developers for the first phase of redevelopment. This phase was planned to create a critical mass and establish the overall character of development by adapting some hospital buildings and developing adjacent parcels with a mix of housing types, plus creating the central plaza and greenway overlook. A total of 211 residential units is recommended. As of October 17, 2005, the agency's project manager, Joe Cain, reported that the agency has selected and is negotiating contracts with two development companies for development of six tracts identified for Phase I of the redevelopment project. Direct Development, based in Wisconsin, and Streuver Bros., Eccels and Rouse of Baltimore, will develop 300 to 500 residential units with complementary retail and office space. The sites are centered in the former hospital area. Cain expects them to break ground by mid-2006.

In addition, the agency has completed designs and initiated a $9 million project to improve infrastructure systems in the first phase area. Selective demolition of hospital structures and abatement of environmental problems to preserve the two wings and power plant have begun.

References:

Author's telephone interviews with Bill Caldwell of RTKL, January 21 and February 2, 2005; and with Joe Cain of the Metropolitan Development and Housing Agency, February 2 and October 17, 2005.

Rolling Mill Hill: A Plan for New Development in Rutledge Hill, Nashville, Tennessee. Prepared by RTKL Associates, Inc., for the Metropolitan Development and Housing Agency, 2003.

"Rolling Mill Hill" project description, from the Agency's Web site: www.nashville.gov/mdha/rolling_mill_hill.htm.

Case Study

Village at Empire Pass Ski Resort, Park City, Utah

The developer of a ski resort organized a citizens' support group and a public information campaign to rebuff a petition drive against the development.

With the local press hostile to a proposed ski resort expansion, moneyed opponents threatening referendum petitions to stopp the project, and the appearance of overwhelming public opposition, the United Park City Mines Company initiated a community outreach effort that successfully combined an opinion survey with grassroots organizing to win approval for their project.

THE SETTING

Park City, Utah, situated in the foothills of the Wasatch Range outside Salt Lake City, is becoming a notable destination for skiers. Deer Valley, Alta, and several other ski resorts have been developed in mountains around Park City, and others are on the drawing boards. The United Park City Mining Company, which owns vast amounts of land from the area's mining days, proposed to build a top-quality, 1,800-acre ski resort on the lower slopes of Flagstaff Mountain, a 10,530-foot peak in Summit County adjoining the Park City municipal boundary. The plan for development included ski slopes and a golf course, a hotel with retail shops and restaurants, mountain biking and hiking trails, a gondola linking downtown Park City with the resort, 54 single-family houses, and 470 multifamily apartments.

The company was pursuing annexation to gain the use of city services. Prevention of annexation would have required the company to initiate entitlement proceedings with the county, with a consequent setback of months or years in initiation of the project. The company believed that city annexation would generate substantial increases in the city's tax base and allow the city to control the development quality of the project.

CARG—Citizens Allied for Reasonable Growth—a well-organized citizens group with a track record of stopping growth and winning elections in Park City, staked out a strong position against the resort plan. CARG presented a real threat to the ski resort because, in a town of just 5,000 voters, CARG needed a mere 1,002 signatures to put a referendum on the ballot to stop the annexation of the resort property into Park City. The United Park City Mining Company turned to GCA Strategies, Inc., a community relations firm based in San Francisco, for advice on ways to counter the petition drive.

Protecting Park City's Quality of Life

Annexation of Flagstaff Mountain will help protect Park City's quality of life by preserving views, reducing traffic impacts, and improving public access. But without annexation, these protections could be at risk since Park City will not be able to control impacts from development and will not receive all the benefits.

Since development is allowed under the general plan of this privately-owned site (as well as under Summit and Wasatch County Zoning), the city's plan for annexation contains strong protection standards.

Annexation will:

Preserve Views: Under Park City's control, placement of housing is designed to protect views. To preserve views from outside Flagstaff Mountain looking in, new single family homes will be restricted to a small portion of the site and will generally be tightly clustered below the ridgeline. While a few Prospector Ridge rooftops may be glimpsed from the Marsac Building area, most homes will not be visible from Old Town at all.

Reduce Traffic Impacts: Under the annexation agreement, the Mines Company will build a $5 million high-speed gondola to convey riders from Main street to Flagstaff Mountain stops within 11 minutes, significantly reducing traffic from the new resort to homes. More important, the gondola system will also reduce existing traffic by connecting Park City Mountain Resort to Deer Valley Resort for the first time. Other transportation improvements required as part of annexation are also designed to help resolve traffic bottlenecks.

Create Public Trails: On what is now private property, annexation will provide legal access to more than 20 miles of trails for public use, including snow-shoeing, skiing and hiking. For the first time, this private land will be made permanently and legally accessible via public trials. The current trail design also includes plans to tie the Flagstaff Mountain trail system into Deer Valley and Park City Mountain Resort's extensive trail systems.

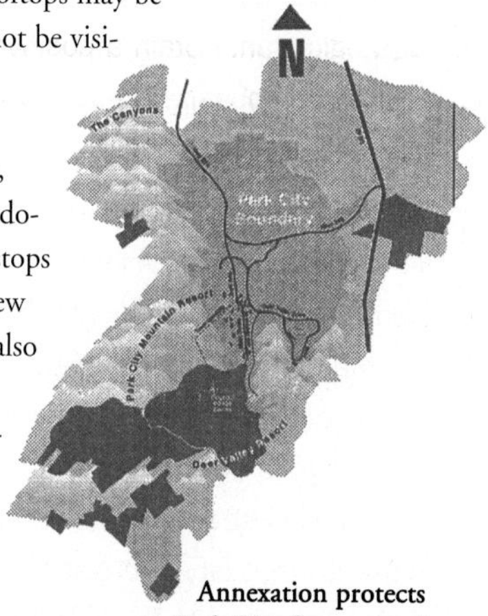

Annexation protects Park City from sprawl.
An area nearly equal in size to that of Park City (6,500 acres) will be protected from over-development through annexation. The area in green above shows nearly 5,000 acres of Mining Company land that will be covered under the annexation agreement, including 93 percent that will be permanently protected as open space. Additionally, annexation will discourage development of 650-1,000 housing units around Park City (off map) by other property owners in nearby Wasatch County.

THE COMMUNITY OUTREACH CAMPAIGN

In this charged political environment, GCA proposed a different route to community agreement than the design-oriented processes described in the other case studies. This was a community conflict over whether the development should be allowed in the community or not. Opposition to the project hinged on CARG's belief that Park City citizens were overwhelmingly against the annexation. As a firm specializing in providing services to shape citizen attitudes and obtain positive actions on proposed projects, GCA saw a need for demonstrating that a considerable proportion of informed citizens would support the development and the annexation. GCA's strategy was to change the perception of who had "the clout" from project opponents to project supporters.

GCA began with a telephone survey of 401 Park City residents to determine just what aspects of the proposed development were worrying local citizens. The survey revealed significant misperceptions about the project, including the misperception that most Park City residents opposed it. The survey also highlighted several positive messages about economic benefits, open space easements, and local control over development that could spark support for the project.

Armed with the survey results and findings from face-to-face interviews with community opinion-leaders, GCA advised the United Park City Mountain Company to undertake a four-point strategic plan: obtain a positive messenger; focus on persuasive messages; spread the word; and emphasize the reality of community support. Overall, the strategy was to create an opportunity to educate local citizens about the project and become advocates for it.

GCA recommended the formation of a citizens' group to demonstrate the extent of community support for the proposed development. Thanks to the mining company's century-old history of community involvement, it was able to quickly mobilize friends and allies to organize a supportive coalition, Park City Citizens for Local Control. This group helped local citizens become familiar with the project, and its leaders became the key spokespeople advocating for the resort. Eventually the group numbered almost 200, more than twice as many as the core group in CARG.

The survey revealed many opposition messages that were popular but not persuasive. While many people believed the project would create traffic problems, rebutting that belief would not materially change attitudes about annexation. On the other hand, several messages were quite persuasive if they could be viewed as credible. Therefore, in spreading the word, proannexation advocates focused on several highly persuasive benefits of the proposed resort development for Park City:

- Annexation would allow Park City rather than the county to control the quality of the development;
- The project would generate new jobs and tax revenues that would flow to the city to help pay for police, fire, and other public services;
- The company was willing to place 88 percent of the land in a conservation easement rather than the 60 percent required by the county.

With CARG disseminating misinformation along with their referendum petitions, it was crucial that voters be properly informed about the qualities of the ski resort and the benefits that would accrue from it. GCA helped the pro-project citizens' group form "truth squads," and held coffees, merchant walks, and other visible events to provide clear, accurate information about the proposal before voters signed opponents' petitions. The coalition's in-person advocacy was also supported by direct mail flyers and newspaper articles that pointed out the benefits of the project to Park City voters. These activities clearly demonstrated the extent of community commitment to the project, significantly reduced the enthusiasm of CARG volunteers, and slowed the rate of signature collection on the referendum petition.

To provide more information about the project, GCA recommended opening a public outreach office in the center of the business district most likely to benefit from the ski resort. The mining company also hosted a series of open houses and ski tours to allow citizens to view the site and learn more about the project. These events showcased the open space to be preserved, highlighted future project benefits and, as a special enticement, included highly prized tours of the historic mine on the property.

Proannexation advocates were given the support they needed to send letters to the editor, telephone their elected officials, testify at public hearings, and recruit their friends and neighbors to attend hearings. The supporter coalition also launched its own petition drive, collecting the names of hundreds of new supporters who not only would be unlikely to sign the CARG petition but who could then be mobilized for other support activities. For example, the coalition went on to stage public rallies that garnered additional press attention about popular support for the resort project.

THE OUTCOME

In a few short weeks of grassroots organizing, Park City Citizens for Local Control and the mining company were able to demonstrate impressive citizen support for the ski resort annexation, despite the protests of slow-growth opponents. The strong citizen support both strengthened the resolve of the city council to support annexation and weakened the influence of CARG. As a result, CARG indicated a new willingness to negotiate modifications of project design and densities rather than deny annexation. At the end of the day, after some alterations in the locations and sizes of some single-family home lots, the city council approved the use permit and annexation.

References:

Author's telephone interviews with Frank Noto of GCA Strategies, Inc., February 4 and 8, 2005, and comments by Noto and GCA president Debra Stein on the draft case study.

Flyers promoting support for the proposed development produced by United Park City Mining Company, 2004.

Part VII Conclusions

Smart growth principles call for involvement of the community in decisions about the character of community development. As described in these pages, involvement by residents can take many forms. Outreach processes have been used extensively by public agencies involved in planning for future development and redevelopment. City planners in many cities, towns, and counties routinely organize discussions about how and where communities should grow. Best of all, citizen involvement in these discussions has led to solutions that in the end, everybody could live with.

ALMOST EVERY PROJECT HAS ITS SHARE of prickly adversaries, and not all of these can be brought around by even the most well-coordinated, heartfelt community engagement process. That said, outreach can and does help to disarm hostile attitudes and build support for proposed development. Approaches vary, but all feature collaborative, interactive discussion and employ a variety of successful techniques and tools for reaching decisions about development strategies, policies, and designs. Many planning and design consulting firms are experts in all kinds of methods for gaining community acceptance for proposed development.

Developers can benefit from this body of knowledge and experience to fashion their own approaches to community engagement. Bob Brugh in Missoula knew what he wanted to develop, and believed that obtaining community support would help in gaining public approval of his project. He hired a consulting firm to organize and manage a community participation process toward the attainment of that goal. In other cases, developers have benefited from the efforts of public agencies to garner community support through collaborative planning for large-scale building projects. The densities and qualities of development approved through these public processes often exceed anything that individual developers might achieve, and provide the policy framework that allows multiple developers to respond to market needs.

The lesson from these experiences is that community engagement processes, done right, build advocacy for smart development. The following keys to success in community engagement can help developers frame effective approaches that result in win/win outcomes:

- **Seek to understand community and citizen concerns:** Define and consider their aspirations, values, fears, and anxieties about development. Recognize that your project may affect many communities with different views and concerns.

Provide leadership for outreach: Make your commitment to collaborative decision making known and visible to the community *before* key decisions have been made. Use interactive tools and techniques to obtain citizen input and feedback to your ideas.

Build trust and ownership: Strive to build a sense of trust between leaders and participants as well as among the participants. Do not make false assurances or raise false hopes. Win participants' belief in and ultimate support for the concepts and plans for development by encouraging them to make suggestions on projects.

Expect to educate: Participants who know little about community development will need to understand what planning is all about—how physical, social, and economic systems interrelate, the ways in which design can alleviate problems, and other aspects of contemporary community building.

Establish a positive vision: Accentuate the positive in your plan and how it will benefit individuals and the community. Make development an opportunity rather than a problem.

Establish clear and reasonable goals and principles: Let participants know what they are working toward—what goals the process can hope to accomplish. Determine some broad principles to guide progress toward the goals. These statements can become milestones for resolving issues and reaching agreements.

Test feasibility and practicality from time to time: Keep plans and designs within the bounds of reality by occasionally testing their market, financial, regulatory, and political feasibility through studies or checkpoints with leadership.

Find win/win solutions or tradeoffs of benefits to resolve issues: Avoid up-or-down votes on controversial issues; instead, negotiate solutions that are beneficial for both the project and the community.

Document every step of the process: To retain the value of the outreach process, document what got done, who did it, and what agreements were reached. Let the community know what has been accomplished through newsletters and other media so that progress is visible. This builds ownership, trust, and support for the outcome.

Processes that inventively engage citizens in thinking and making decisions about development create community trust and appreciation for the products of development—a boon to the community at large as well as individual project developers.

References:

Godschalk, David R.: et al. *Pulling Together: A Planning and Development Consensus-Building Manual.* Washington, D.C.: Urban Land Institute, 1994.

Kobza, Kim Patrick. *There Goes the Neighborhood: Protecting Your Home and Community from Poor Development Choices.* Naples, Florida: Neighborhood American Press, 1998.

Merriam, Dwight H. *The Complete Guide to Zoning.* New York: McGraw Hill, 2004.

Moore, C. Nicholas, and Dave Davis. *Participation Tools for Better Land-Use Planning,* 2nd ed. Sacramento: Center for Livable Communities, 1997.

Stein, Debra. *Winning Community Support for Land Use Projects.* Washington, D.C.: Urban Land Institute, 1992.

Schreiber, Kenneth, Gary Binger, and Dennis Church. *Higher Density Plans: Tools for Community Engagement.* Published online by the Mineta Transportation Institute in the College of Business at San Jose State University, San Jose, California, at http://transweb.sjsu.edu/publications/03-02/mti_03-02.pdf, August 2004.

Thomsett, Michael C. *NIMBYism: Navigating the Politics of Local Opposition.* Arlington, Virginia: Centerline Publishing, 2004.